**Women
Explorers**

Gertrude Bell
Explorer of the Middle East

Women Explorers

Women
Explorers

Gertrude Bell
Explorer of the Middle East

Heather Lehr Wagner

Introduction: Milbry Polk,
author of *Women of Discovery*

CHELSEA HOUSE
PUBLISHERS
A Haights Cross Communications Company
Philadelphia

CHELSEA HOUSE PUBLISHERS

VP, NEW PRODUCT DEVELOPMENT Sally Cheney
DIRECTOR OF PRODUCTION Kim Shinners
CREATIVE MANAGER Takeshi Takahashi
MANUFACTURING MANAGER Diann Grasse

Staff for GERTRUDE BELL

ASSOCIATE EDITOR Kate Sullivan
PRODUCTION EDITOR Megan Emery
PHOTO EDITOR Sarah Bloom
SERIES & COVER DESIGNER Terry Mallon
LAYOUT 21st Century Publishing and Communications, Inc.

A Haights Cross Communications ✦ Company

http://www.chelseahouse.com

First Printing

9 8 7 6 5 4 3 2 1

Library of Congress Cataloging-in-Publication Data

Wagner, Heather Lehr.
   Gertrude Bell : explorer of the Middle East/by Heather Lehr Wagner.
      v. cm.—(Women explorers)
Includes bibliographical references and index.
Contents: The mark of the desert—Childhood memories—The colors
of the East—The voice of the wind—The romance of the desert—
Intelligence officer—A new nation—Stateswoman and advisor.
   ISBN 0-7910-7711-X
   1. Saudi Arabia—Description and travel—Juvenile literature. 2. Bell,
Gertrude Lowthian, 1868-1926—Travel—Saudi Arabia—Juvenile
literature. [1. Bell, Gertrude Lowthian, 1868-1926. 2. Travelers.
3. Stateswomen. 4. Women—Biography. 5. Middle East—Description
and travel.] I. Title. II. Series.
DS208.W34 2004
956'.02'092—dc22

                                                    2003026136

Table of Contents

Introduction

By Milbry Polk

Curiosity is one of the most compelling forces of human life. Our desire to understand who and what and where we are drives us restlessly to explore and to comprehend what we see. Every historical era is known by the individuals who sought to expand our boundaries of time and space and knowledge. People such as Alexander the Great, Ibn Battuta, Marco Polo, Ferdinand Magellan, Hernando de Soto, Meriwether Lewis, William Clark, Charles Darwin, Sir Richard Burton, Roald Amundsen, Jacques Cousteau, Edmund Hillary, Tenzing Norgay, Thor Hyerdahl, and Neil Armstrong are men whose discoveries changed our world-view. They were explorers, leaders into the unknown. This series is about a handful of individuals who have been left out of the history books but whose feats loom large, whose discoveries changed the way we look at the world. They are women explorers.

WHAT MAKES SOMEONE AN EXPLORER?

The desire to know what lies beyond the next hill—the desire to explore—is one of the most powerful of human impulses. This drive makes us unique among the species with which we share our earth. Curiosity helped to impel our remote ancestors out of Africa. It is what spread them in waves throughout the world where they settled; curiosity helped them adapt to the many environments they encountered.

Myths of all cultures include the memories of early explorations. These myths were the means by which people explained to themselves and taught their children about life, about the world around them, and about death. Myths helped people make sense of the inexplicable forces of nature and the strangeness of new lands and peoples. The few myths and legends that have come down to us are the stories of early exploration.

What makes someone an explorer? The qualities required are not unique. We are born explorers. Every child, even in the crib, is reaching out, trying to understand, to take the measure of its own body, then its immediate surroundings, and we continue as we go through life to grasp ever-widening circles of experience and reality. As we grow up, we often lose the excitement of the child, the characteristic that supposedly gave Albert Einstein his ability to see the universe in a new way. What typifies the explorer is not losing this wonderful childlike curiosity. He or she still reaches out. Explorers are open minded—able to look at and accept what they see, rather than to fall back upon pre-conceived notions. Explorers are courageous, not just in facing physical danger, but also in having the courage to confront failure, ridicule, and laughter, and yet to keep on going. Above all, explorers have the ability to communicate. All insights, observations, and discoveries mean nothing to the wider community if they are not documented and shared. An explorer goes out into the world at some personal risk and discovers something of value and then shares that knowledge with his or her community. Explorers are leaders who look at the world in new ways and in doing so make breakthroughs that enrich all of our lives.

WOMEN EXPLORERS

Women, like men, have always been explorers. Typically in a "hunter-gatherer" society the men hunted animals while the women ventured far from the camps in search of other foods. Though their tasks were different, both were explorers. And, since such societies were almost constantly on the move, women were there for each voyage of discovery. But over time, as cultural groups became more settled, ideas began to change about the role of women in society. Women came to be restricted to the house, the shared courtyard, or the village and began to wear clothing that set them apart. By the time of the Middle Ages often the only way women in the Western world could travel was by going on pilgrimage. The trek to visit holy sites offered women one of the few opportunities to see new places, hear new languages, and meet different people. In fact, the first autobiography in the English language was written by a pilgrim, Margery Kempe (1373–1440), about her journeys throughout Europe and to the Holy Land.

Over time, women became formally excluded from exploration. Of course, some women did manage to find a way around the obstacles. Those who did venture forth went alone or in disguise and often needed men to help them. But their stories were not recorded in official histories; to find their stories one has to dig deep.

About three hundred years ago, the western worldview changed. Beginning in the 1700s, the scientific revolution began to change life for everyone in Europe. Men as well as women were swept up in the excitement to classify and understand every aspect of life on earth. Legions of people went to every corner of the world to see and record what was there. The spirit of adventure began to find new means of expression. New modes of transportation made movement around the world easier and new technologies made recording events and communication less expensive and more vivid.

The findings of these explorers were fascinating to the people back home. Wealthy individuals collected many of the strange insects, botanical specimens, native art, rocks, and other findings, brought back by the explorers into personal collections called Cabinets of Curiosities. These Cabinets of

Curiosities are the forerunners of our modern museums. The desire to collect the unusual financed expeditions, which in turn fostered public interest in exploration. The creation and spread of scientific and popular magazines with stories about expeditions and discoveries enabled the public to learn about the world. By the 1800s, explorers had the status of popular heroes in the public eye. The lure of the unknown gripped society.

Unlike men, women did not have support of institutions such as universities, museums, scientific societies, governments, and the military that sponsored and financed exploration. Until well into the twentieth century, many of these institutions barred women from participation, membership, and especially leadership. Women were thought capable of gathering things such as flowers or rocks for subjects to paint and draw, but men were the ones who studied them, named them, and published books about them. Most women, if they had any specialized education at all, gained it through private tutors. Men went to the university. Men formed and joined scientific societies and the exploring clubs. Men ran the governments, the military, and the press, and archived the collections. Universities and other cultural institutions were open only to the membership of men. Women were generally excluded from them. When these institutions sponsored exploration, they sponsored men. Women not only had to overcome mountains in the wild but also institutions at home.

In the 1800s women were not usually trained or taught academics. Instead, they learned sewing, music, and how to behave as a lady. A woman who managed to learn to write overcame great obstacles. Few managed to do it, but the same spirit that made women into explorers animated their minds in other ways. A few women learned to record what they were doing sufficiently well that at least some of their works have become classics of description and adventure.

Because of them, we know the little we do know about their lives and actions. As the nineteenth century progressed, more and more women were going out collecting, recording, and writing about faraway places. By the late 1800s more women were educated and those who traveled often wrote accounts of their journeys. So, now, in the twenty-first century, we are just beginning to learn about the unknown side of exploration—the women's story—from the accounts that lay buried in our archives.

And what a story it is. For example, one of the first modern women explorers was Maria Sybila Merian, who sailed to Surinam in 1699 at the age of 52. Not content to view the strange flora and fauna that were arriving back in Europe to fill the Cabinets of Curiosity, she wanted to collect and paint insects and animals in their native habitat.

Western women also faced societal obstacles; they generally could not go anywhere without a chaperon. So for a would-be woman explorer, a night in the wild spent in the company of a man who was not a close relative or her husband was unthinkable. And then there were the unsuitable clothes. In many parts of the early modern world it was punishable by death (as it was in Spain in the 1600s) or imprisonment (as it was in America well into the late 1800s) for women to appear in public wearing pants.

The heavy, layered dresses and tight corsets thought necessary for women made traveling very cumbersome. For example, when the Alps began to be climbed by explorers in the 1800s, a few women were caught up in the mania. The first two women to summit the Matterhorn climbed in skirts and corsets. The third woman, an American professor of Latin, Annie Smith Peck (1850–1935), realized the absurdity of leaping crevasses, climbing ice walls, and enduring the winds in a skirt. So, she wore pants. This created such a sensation in 1895 that the Singer Sewing

Machine Company photographed her and included a card with her in climbing gear with every machine it sold.

THE WOMEN EXPLORERS SERIES

When asked why he wanted to climb Mount Everest, George Mallory famously replied "Because it's there." Perhaps another explorer would answer the same question, "Because I don't know what is there and I want to find out."

Although we all have curiosity, what separates explorers is their willingness to take their curiosity further. Despite the odds, a lack of money, and every imaginable difficulty, they still find a way to go. They do so because they are passionate about life and their passion carries them over the barriers. As you will discover, the women profiled in this series shared that passion. Their passion gave them the strength to face what would seem to be insurmountable odds to most of us. To read their stories is more than learning about the adventure, it is a guide to discovering our own passions. The women in this series, Mary Kingsley, Gertrude Bell, Alexandra David-Néel, Annie Montague Alexander, Sue Hendrickson, and Sylvia Earle, all join the pantheon of explorers, the heroes of our age.

These six women have been chosen because their interests range from geographical to cultural exploration; from traversing the highest mountains to diving to the depths of the oceans; from learning about life far back in time to looking forward into the future. These women are extraordinary leaders and thinkers. They are all individuals who have braved the unknown and challenged the traditional women's roles. Their discoveries have had remarkable and profound effects on what we know about the world. To be an explorer one does not have to be wealthy or have multiple degrees. To be an explorer one must have the desire from within and focus on the destination: the unknown.

Mary Kingsley (1862–1900) was the daughter of an English Victorian gentleman-explorer who believed women did not need to be educated. Mary was kept at home and only tutored in German to translate articles her father wanted to read. But while he was away, she went into his library and educated herself by reading his books. She never married and followed the custom of her day for unmarried women by staying home with her parents. When her parents died she found herself alone—and suddenly free. She purchased a ticket to the Canary Islands with her inheritance. Once there, she learned about the Congo, then considered by the Europeans to be a terrifying place. When Kingsley decided to go to the Congo, she was warned that all she would find would be festering swamplands laced with deadly diseases and cannibals. Kingsley viewed that warning as a challenge. Having used up all her money on the ticket, she outfitted herself as a trader. She returned to the Congo, and in a wooden canoe she plied the tributaries of the Congo River, trading goods with the natives and collecting fish for the British Museum. She learned the languages of the interior and befriended the local tribes. She became an expert on their rich belief systems, which were completely unknown in Europe. Like many explorers, Mary Kingsley's knowledge bridged separate worlds, helping each understand and appreciate the other.

Gertrude Bell (1868–1926) was the daughter of a wealthy English industrialist. She had tremendous ambition, which she used to convince her parents to give her an education at a time when, for a woman, education was considered secondary to a good marriage. As a result of her intelligence and determination, she won one of the few coveted spots for women at Oxford University. After college, she did not know what to do. Girls of her class usually waited at home for a proposal of marriage. But after Bell returned home, she received an invitation from her uncle to visit Persia (modern-day Iran). Quickly, she set about learning Persian. Later she learned Arabic and begin her own archeological trips into the Syrian deserts.

When World War I broke out, Bell was in the Middle East. Her ability to speak the language, as well as her knowledge of the local tribes and the deserts from her archeological work, caused the British to appoint her to one of the most important jobs in the Desert War, that of Oriental Secretary. The Oriental Secretary was the officer of the embassy who was expected to know about and deal with local affairs, roughly what we call a political officer in an embassy. Bell played a major role in crafting the division of the Middle East into the countries we know today. She also founded the museum in Iraq.

Alexandra David-Néel (1868–1969) was performing in the Paris Opera when she married a banker. As she now had some financial freedom, she decided to act on her lifelong dream to travel to the East. Soon after she married, she sailed alone for India. She assured her husband she be gone only about 18 months; it would be 24 years before she would return home. Upon arriving in India she became intrigued with the Buddhist religion. She felt in order to understand Buddhism, she had first to master Tibetan, the language in which many of the texts were written. In the course of doing so, she plunged so deeply into the culture that she became a Buddhist nun. After several years of study, David-Néel became determined to visit the home of the spiritual leader of the Tibetan Buddhists, the Dalai Lama, who resided in the Holy City of Lhasa, in Tibet. This was quite a challenge because all foreigners were forbidden from entering Lhasa. At the age of 55, she began a long and arduous winter trek across the Himalayas toward Tibet. She succeeded in becoming the first Western woman to visit Lhasa. After returning to France, David-Néel dedicated the rest of her long life to helping Westerners understand the beauty and complexity of Buddhist religion and culture through her many writings.

A wealthy and restless young woman, Annie Montague Alexander (1867–1950) decided to pursue her interests in science and nature rather than live the life of a socialite in San Francisco. She organized numerous expeditions throughout the American West to collect flora, fauna, and fossils. Concerned by the rapid changes occurring due to the growing population, Alexander envisaged a time, all too soon, when much of the natural world of the West would be gone due to urbanization and agricultural development. As a tribute to the land she loved, she decided to create the best natural history museum of the American West. She actually created two museums at the University of California, Berkeley, in which to house the thousands of specimens she had assembled. In the course of her exploration, she discovered new species, seventeen of which are named for her. Though little known, Alexander contributed much to our knowledge of American zoology and paleontology.

Two women in this series are still actively exploring. Sue Hendrickson dropped out of high school and made a living by collecting fish off the Florida Keys to sell to aquariums. An invitation to go on an underwater dive trip changed her life. She became passionate about diving, and soon found herself working with archeologists on wrecks. Hendrickson was often the lead diver, diving first to find out what was there. She realized she had a knack for seeing things others missed. On land, she became an amber collector of pieces of fossilized resin that contained insects and later became a dinosaur hunter. While on a fossil expedition in the Badlands of the Dakotas, Hendrickson discovered the largest *Tyrannosaurus rex* ever found. It has been named Sue in her honor. Depending on the time of year, she can be found diving in the sunken ancient port of Alexandria, Egypt, mapping Spanish wrecks off Cuba's coastline, or in the high, dry lands of ancient forests hunting for dinosaur bones.

Sylvia Earle began her exploration of the sea in the early days of scuba. Smitten with the undersea world, she earned degrees in biology and oceanography. She wanted more than to just study the sea; she wanted to live in the sea. In the early 1970s, Earle was eager to take part in a project in which humans lived in a module underwater for extended periods of time for the U.S. Navy. Unfortunately, when the project was about to begin, she was informed that because she was a woman, she could not go. Undaunted, Earle designed the next phase of the project exclusively for women. This project had far-reaching results. It proved to the U.S. military that women could live well in a confined environment and opened the door for women's entry into the space program.

Earle, ever reaching for new challenges, began designing and testing submersibles, which would allow a human to experience the underwater world more intimately than anything created up to that time. Approaching age 70, her goal is to explore the deepest, darkest place on earth: the 35,800-foot-deep Marianas Trench south of Guam, in the Pacific Ocean.

The experiences of these six women illustrate different paths, different experiences, and different situations, but each led to a similar fulfillment in exploration. All are explorers; all have given us the gift of understanding some aspect of our world. All offer tremendous opportunities to us. Each of us can learn from them and follow in their paths. They are trailblazers; but many trails remain unexplored. There is so much unknown about the world, so much that needs to be understood. For example, less than 5 percent of the ocean has been explored. Thousands of species of plants and animals wait to be discovered. We have not reached every place on earth, and of what we have seen, we often understand very little. Today, we are embarked on the greatest age of exploration. And we go armed with more knowledge than any of the explorers who have gone before us.

What these women teach us is that we need explorers to help us understand what is miraculous in the world around us. The goal for each of us is to find his or her own path and begin the journey.

1

The Mark
of the Desert

In November 1913, a 45-year-old Englishwoman named Gertrude Bell set sail for the Middle East. It was not her first trip to that part of the world. Bell had spent much of her life in search of adventure, and she had become quite famous in the Middle East for her knowledge of the region; her fluency in Arabic, Persian, and other languages; and her valuable contacts among the people who lived there.

Since the turn of the century, when she traveled to visit friends in Jerusalem in the area then known as Palestine, the region had fascinated her. She became a skilled linguist and published a critically acclaimed translation of Persian poetry. She traveled to Persia (now known as Iran), to Syria, and to the area we now know as Iraq. Only one region had eluded her for years: Arabia.

The vast desert that spread across the heart of the Arabian Peninsula was largely controlled by two rival sheikhs: Ibn Rashid and Ibn Saud. For years, their families had fought for control of central Arabia. In 1891, the Rashid clan defeated the Saudis and forced them into exile in Kuwait. There, living in relative poverty, the Saudis had plotted their return to Arabia and to power. By 1904, their plotting turned to action. The young Ibn Saud led a small group of 15 of his clansmen back into Arabia. Under cover of darkness, they climbed over the walls of the Rashid city of Riyadh and quickly seized control. For the next few years, the Rashids and Saudis continued their history of warfare, battling for control of Arabia.

PLANNING THE JOURNEY

On several previous occasions, Gertrude Bell's plans to visit Arabia had been thwarted by the two battling sheikhs and those tribes allied with them. The conditions were too dangerous for anyone to gain safe passage through the territory. Moreover, Bell's plans were much more ambitious than simply traveling through the Arabian Desert. She hoped to meet the leaders of the two warring tribes, Ibn Rashid and Ibn Saud. Determined to realize this hope, she decided to make the trip despite the dangers. Gertrude Bell arrived in Damascus on November 27, 1913, following a difficult, multistage journey from England. She traveled by boat to France, sailed across the Mediterranean aboard another boat, and finally traveled

IBN SAUD

Gertrude Bell sensed that Ibn Saud could be a critical ally for Great Britain in Arabia. Her belief that he was a powerful force in the region proved correct.

Ibn Saud grew up in exile, his once powerful family forced from their land first by the Ottoman Turks and later by the Rashid tribe. As a teenager, Abdul Aziz Ibn Saud lived among Bedouin nomads, learning from them to sleep under the stars and live without luxuries. His family later moved to an impoverished area of Kuwait. As Ibn Saud grew older, he vowed to avenge his family and recapture the land they once held.

At the age of 21, he led an attack on the Rashid city of Riyadh. With a force of only 60 men armed with just a few rifles, swords, and daggers, he led a surprise attack and captured the city. Following this success, he built alliances with Bedouin tribesmen and gradually added to his territory, eventually capturing the holy cities of Mecca and Medina, until all of the Arabian Peninsula was in Saudi hands.

At various points, British representatives had the opportunity to ally themselves with Ibn Saud, but they more often chose to back his rivals, including Ibn Rashid and Sharif Hussein. Ibn Saud would gain control of Arabia— and the rich oil resources that were discovered there— thanks to his own courage and military skills and because of his alliances with various tribes. Descendants of Ibn Saud rule the Arabian Peninsula to this day.

by train from Beirut to Damascus. She heard in Damascus that conditions in Arabia had improved; the Rashids and Saudis seemed to be relatively quiet, and a trip into the desert seemed possible.

Bell arrived in Damascus equipped with items that she felt were necessary for her journey. Inside her large steamer trunk were several fashionable French gowns and skirts, fur coats for the chilly winter weather, tweed jackets, fringed shawls, frilly blouses, plumed hats, parasols, and linen riding clothes. She had silver brushes and cut-glass containers holding creams and lotions, crates containing Wedgwood china, crystal stemware, silver flatware, table linens, rugs, and several volumes of Shakespeare and history and archeology texts. She brought with her guidebooks, quinine, camphor, boric ointment, a remedy for diarrhea, bandages, soaps, and flea powder. She also had a separate suitcase that was designed to embarrass anyone who might search her luggage—an upper layer of lacy petticoats and corsets hid maps, cameras, film, binoculars, bullets, and guns.[1]

Bell quickly made plans to travel to Hayil, Ibn Rashid's capital, before continuing on to meet with Ibn Saud. She wrote to her father, requesting additional funds to cover the expense of the journey. She needed 17 camels, food, presents to hand out on the journey—things like cloaks, *keffeyehs* (head coverings), and cotton cloth—all of which were more easily obtained in Damascus than in the desert through which she would be traveling. Because it was common for travelers to encounter bandits along the way, she was afraid to carry too much cash with her on the journey. Instead, she deposited a large sum of money with an Arabian merchant in Damascus and obtained from him a line of credit that she would draw upon when she reached Hayil. She assured her father that she would pay him back with money earned from the sale of the book she planned to write about her journey.

The first obstacle came quickly: The faithful guide who had accompanied her on previous journeys, a young man named Fattuh, became sick. Bell decided to postpone the journey until he recovered, but what was initially believed to be malaria was later diagnosed as typhoid, and she was eventually forced to depart without him.

Gertrude Bell left Damascus on December 16, 1913 and rapidly discovered how unfortunate it was to be without Fattuh. The men who had been hired to accompany her had never traveled with a European before. They did not know how Bell's English tents were to be erected or dismantled. They did not know how to pack and unpack her luggage or to prepare her meals. Bell quickly took charge, instructing them in how she would like things done and firmly demonstrating that she was leading the expedition. She was unlike any woman they had ever met before.

Heavy rain and winds further complicated the journey. The first morning, the combination of rain and unfamiliar equipment caused the process of breaking up the camp to take a full two and a half hours. Soon, Bell reduced this time by an hour.

The temperatures were very cold, and the water the travelers found in the early days of their journey was little more than pools of muddy rainwater. Luckily, Bell had brought drinking water with her from Damascus to sustain her and her team. She had also brought bread, meat, and eggs. Bell found the early stages of the journey dreary—her team could not travel when it rained heavily because the camels would slip and fall in the mud. On such days, she sat cold and wet in her camp for hours, sewing bags to hold the camp's provisions and occasionally venturing out to map the region.

In spite of these delays, Bell loved the desert. She felt more at home in its vastness and emptiness than she did in the bustling streets of London. The strict codes that governed behavior and left few options for women in

England did not exist for those few Europeans who ventured into the Middle East. It was a different, magical world. In a letter to her stepmother, written on December 20, 1913, she wrote of feeling once more as if the desert were her own place:

> . . . silence and solitude fall round you like an impenetrable veil; there is no reality but the long hours of riding, shivering in the morning and drowsy in the afternoon, the bustle of getting into camp, the talk round Muhammad's coffee fire after dinner, profounder sleep than civilization contrives, and then the road again.[2]

THE END OF THE YEAR

For several days, Bell and her servants traveled across the desert, suffering from the cold. At one point, the tent in which her male servants slept froze so solidly that they were forced to light fires under it to defrost the canvas enough so that it could be packed away without tearing. Each morning, the area would be thick with mist, but gradually the sun would rise and break through the fog, warming Bell as she traveled. The heavy rains had prompted grass and shrubs to grow, forming patches along the ground that, in other spots, was covered with volcanic rock.

One day Bell climbed the large volcano at Jebel Sais; she gazed out at the desert, the vast yellow earth, the shining pools of water, and the miles of stones, and she photographed them all. The next day, her expedition was attacked by a group of about a dozen Druze warriors, most of them barely clothed and one completely naked, who galloped on horseback up to the expedition, firing warning shots into the air as they approached. They shrieked and yelled; one even seized Bell's camel and hit it on the neck to make it kneel. They took the revolvers, bullets, and cloaks of Bell's men and threatened and terrified them all. Suddenly they recognized certain members of Bell's party. The seized property was quickly returned, and one of the Druze warriors even offered to accompany Bell to ensure that future attacks were prevented.

Bell spent a cold Christmas Day taking rubbings of various inscriptions she had found—inscriptions that predated the Prophet Muhammad—written by nomadic tribes that had traveled through the deserts. Throughout earlier travels, she had gathered data that had proved valuable to archeologists; she hoped this trip would yield additional valuable research. She made notes for the map she was drafting and took more photographs. As the year drew to a close, the journey became more difficult. The camels marched over mile after mile of stones, and there was little water available. This meant no bathing and as little washing as possible.

Despite the hardships, Bell was happy. After dinner, she enjoyed sitting for an hour or so at the men's camp, warming herself by their fire and listening to stories of their travels through the desert. She could converse easily in Arabic and enjoyed the jokes and tall tales that the relaxed evenings by the campfire inspired.

By January, the land across which Bell traveled had fewer markings by which to measure the distance covered. It was dry and barren. Each time the party came across water, the expedition would halt. Containers were filled up with as much water as possible to carry the party through the days when no water would be available.

In her diary, Bell wrote of the waves of yellow and red sand that stretched around her: "But what a world! The incredible desolation. Abandoned of God and man, that is how it looks— and is. I think no one can travel here and come back the same. It sets its seal upon you, for good or ill."[3]

ACROSS THE DESERT

As the journey led her deeper into the desert, Bell's spirits lifted. She described it vividly:

> . . . real desert as you see it in picture books. It is made of nothing but red sandstone and the resulting red-gold sand. Sometimes the sandstone heaps itself up into a long low ridge and the wind heaps the sand about it into long low hills. Between lie shallow bottoms, *nugrah* they are called, wherein the sandstone lies in floors, with deep sand between, the whole strewn over with mounds of stone, broken and ruined into strange shapes by sun and wind. And here, if you can believe it, the darling spring has not refused to come. The thorny bushes are all grey green against the red gold of the sand and some have even put forth very faintly coloured flowers. In spite of the desolation and the emptiness, it is beautiful—or is it beautiful partly because of the emptiness? At any rate I love it, and though the camels pace so slowly, eating as they go, I feel no impatience and no desire to get to anywhere.[4]

Traveling through the desert was not always so inspiring. Bell occasionally suffered from bouts of depression, worried not by the danger but by whether or not the journey would prove worth it in the end. The slow pace was frustrating for Bell—the expedition was barred from the swiftest routes by hostile tribes or waterless regions. She was also disappointed by the absence of any inscriptions or archeological landmarks worth recording. By February 16, she had noted in her diary that she felt far from being the daughter of kings, a description she had earned earlier. "I almost wish something would happen," she wrote, "—something exciting, a raid or a battle. . . . It's a bore being a woman when you are in Arabia."[5] Bell did not know how prophetic her wish would prove.

PRISONER AT HAYIL

On February 24, Bell camped within sight of Hayil, Ibn Rashid's capital. She had long dreamed of meeting the head of the Rashid family and his rival, the head of the Saud family, and now her journey seemed to have placed her first goal within reach. The Rashid family had been weakened by years of fighting in which one leader after another had been brutally killed. The current Ibn Rashid was only 16 years old, and Bell soon learned that she would not be able to meet him. He was away, leading a warring party in the north, and his uncle, Ibrahim, had been left to govern Hayil in his absence. Contrary to what she had been told in Damascus, the desert was not quiet. The Rashids and Saudis were once more on the march.

On February 25, Bell broke camp and rode towards Hayil. Her men were anxious—the stories of warring parties left them worried about the reception they would receive in the capital. As they neared the city, they were met by three men on camels who welcomed them in the name of Ibrahim. They announced that they would be Bell's servants during her stay, and she was quickly escorted through the gates of the town.

Inside the city walls, Bell was welcomed by another male relative of Ibn Rashid's: his great-uncle Muhammad. She dismounted from her camel and followed Muhammad up a long ramp to an open court. There she was led into a great room whose soaring ceiling was supported by columns. The room was lined with sofas and elegant carpeting.

Gertrude Bell was invited to sit down and rest in this reception room while her men left to pitch tents in the courtyard below and care for the camels. Soon, two women came into the room. One was an old woman named Lu-lu-ah who was dressed in a red cotton robe and a black head covering. She, Bell learned, was the caretaker, and she was followed by another, more elegantly dressed woman named Turkiyyeh who wore bright red and purple cotton robes and long strings of pearls around her neck. The three women were soon chatting in Arabic, and Turkiyyeh gave Bell a tour of the house.

Turkiyyeh shared much of the local gossip with Bell, and Bell, perhaps unwisely, told Turkiyyeh of her plans to journey on from Hayil to visit Ibn Saud. Shortly before this conversation, rumors had reached Hayil that Ibn Saud planned to attack the city, and the Rashids had no intention of letting anyone who might potentially share information with Ibn Saud travel from their city. Bell was informed that she could not leave without permission and had to wait until Ibn Rashid's uncle decided what should be done with her.

For two days Bell waited in the elegant reception room. No one from the Rashid family came to visit her; no one provided her with any information. It was soon clear that she was being held prisoner. Finally, on the evening of the fourth day—women in Hayil were only permitted in the streets after dark—she was escorted by slaves into the palace. Ibrahim and a group of men sat on the carpet. Bell presented them with gifts, and Ibrahim invited her to sit beside him. She was served coffee, and Ibrahim began recounting a bit of the violent history of the Rashid family. Before Bell could bring up the issue of her imprisonment, a servant appeared with an incense holder and swung it three times in front of her—a signal that it was time to leave. Shortly after she returned to her room, the gifts she had presented to Ibrahim returned as well.

Again, Bell paced and waited. Occasionally her servants appeared, bringing her rumors from the town. No one was clear when she would be released. The most important rumor was that the young leader of the Rashid family was busy fighting in the north and had no immediate plans to return to Hayil.

On her sixth morning in captivity, she was allowed to ride with an escort through Ibrahim's gardens. That evening she was again invited to meet with Ibrahim. She explained that she had sold a few camels when she had arrived in Hayil, but that her money was now gone. She told Ibrahim about the line of credit that she had arranged while still in Damascus, a sum that she had been promised would be at her disposal when she arrived in Hayil. Bell noted that she wanted to continue on her journey but that she could not proceed without funds.

Ibrahim replied that it would be quite impossible. No money could be given to her until Ibn Rashid returned—and he was not expected back for a month.

Bell waited for nine long days, repeatedly sending forth requests for her freedom and repeatedly being refused. At last, she was allowed to visit a nearby garden belonging to two young princes who studied her silently as she walked. When she returned to her room, she began to send messages— to Turkiyyeh, to Ibrahim, and to various other members of the Rashid family. She received only the same reply— nothing could be done until Ibn Rashid returned. Rumors reached Bell that an attack on Hayil by the Saudis was imminent. She knew that there was little chance she would survive such an attack.

Finally, on March 6, she was summoned to the tent of the palace's chief eunuch, Said. Said was known to have great influence. In the past, whenever she had encountered anyone of influence, Bell had been careful to speak politely, following the Arabic customs and traditions as closely as possible. By now, however, she was too angry. She strode into Said's tent and demanded her money and her camels, saying that she would leave Hayil at once. Then she stood up quickly and left while the men in the tent were still seated—a great offense. Bell no longer cared.

That evening, Said appeared with a bag of gold coins worth the full amount of her line of credit. Camels also appeared. No explanations or apologies were given, but she was told that she now had permission to leave Hayil. She asked for, and was given, permission to photograph the palace, the marketplace, and even the people around her. Then, after two weeks of imprisonment, she left Hayil.

Bell's journey had come to an unceremonious end. The behavior of the Rashids and the rumors of imminent attacks from the Saudis made it clear that no trip south to meet Ibn Saud would be possible that year. Despite the imprisonment and the disappointment, Bell noted in her journal, "I carry away a deep impression of the beauty and charm of it all—the dustlessness, the silence, with no wheeled vehicles, only the pad of the camels in the soft grit, or of donkeys." [6]

Bell turned back and headed for Baghdad. Warned that the eastern passage was no longer safe, she traveled by the western road, moving nearly ten hours a day across dangerous stretches of land. In about three weeks, she was safely back in Baghdad. She wrote in her journal:

> . . . the end of an adventure always leaves one with a feeling of disillusion—don't you know it? I try to school myself beforehand by reminding myself how I have looked forward and looked forward at other times to the end, and when it came have found it—just nothing. Dust and ashes in one's hand, dead bones that look as if they would never rise and dance—it's all just nothing and one turns away from it with a sigh and tries to fix one's eyes on to the new thing before one. That's how I felt when I came into Baghdad. And this adventure hasn't been successful either. I have not done what I meant to do . . . [7]

The journey into Arabia had ended in failure, but it would not be Bell's only trip into the desert. She would eventually realize her dream of meeting Ibn Saud. She would become one of her country's most valuable resources during the war that would dramatically reshape the region she loved. Ultimately, the nations of the Middle East that would rise up from the ashes of World War I would be dramatically affected by the thoughts and writings of a middle-aged Englishwoman who felt most at home when she was far from home.

2

Childhood Memories

Gertrude Bell's book *The Desert and the Sown* begins with an explanation: "To those bred under an elaborate social order few such moments of exhilaration can come as that which stands at the threshold of wild travel."[8] For Gertrude Bell, the beginning of a new journey, the launching point for what she described as "wild travel," represented a kind of freedom—freedom from the expectations for women of her age, marital status, and class; freedom from the confines of her life in England; and freedom to discover something better and stronger in herself.

Bell, as her book revealed, had been born "under an elaborate social order." Her grandfather, Isaac Lowthian Bell, was one of the wealthiest and most successful men in Newcastle, England. A highly educated man, he had studied chemistry, physics, and metallurgy in Denmark, Scotland, Germany, and France before joining his father's ironworks factory. Lowthian Bell very quickly put to use his knowledge of science in the practical forum of his father's ironworks plant, becoming one of the first manufacturers to use blast furnaces for smelting iron ore. He launched the first aluminum manufacturing plant in England. By 1844, he and his two brothers had created Bell Brothers, a firm whose wide-ranging interests included steel mills, ironstone mines, coal mines, and limestone quarries.

At a time when the British Empire was thriving, in part because of its steel, coal, and iron resources, Bell Brothers became northeast England's largest and most important ironworks and coal-mining firm. The company supplied more than one-third of all the iron used in England and employed more than 47,000 men.[9] Isaac Bell soon translated his manufacturing power into political power. He was elected mayor of Newcastle and sheriff of Durham County and held a seat in Parliament for five years.

Bell's scientific knowledge earned him a place in England's prestigious Fellow of the Royal Society. In 1895, he was honored with the Albert Medal, which was awarded to him in recognition of his metallurgical research and the contributions he had made to the development of the iron and steel industries. As an Albert Medal recipient, he joined an elite group that included Thomas Edison, Queen Victoria, and Louis Pasteur. Isaac Bell loved to travel, spending much time in America; his oldest son, Thomas Hugh Bell (known as Hugh), shared his love of learning and travel.

The Bell household was often visited by many of the men who helped shape the nineteenth century. As a boy, Hugh Bell might find Charles Darwin or Thomas Huxley having dinner with his parents. Isaac Bell, despite his wealth and success, also invited many of the social reformers of the Victorian Age to his home and listened to their ideas of how industrialists must adopt a position of social responsibility to help those less fortunate.

Like his father, Hugh Bell was well educated and well traveled at an early age. He studied chemistry, organic chemistry, and mathematics, and he attended schools in Scotland, France, and Germany. He soon joined Bell Brothers and contributed to the firm's success in coal and iron manufacture, but his passion was secondary education. Hugh Bell founded Middlesbrough High School and championed the causes of improving public education and health and creating child welfare laws targeting firms that placed children in dangerous working conditions.

When he was 23 years old, Hugh Bell married Mary Shield, the daughter of a Newcastle food merchant. The newlyweds moved into the Bell family home. The impressive estate, known as Washington Hall, had been built by Isaac Bell in 1854. It was here that Hugh and Mary Bell's first child was born on July 14, 1868, a girl named Gertrude Margaret Lowthian Bell.

EARLIEST DAYS

As a toddler, Gertrude Bell enjoyed a privileged life, surrounded by doting family members and an attentive nanny. The little girl, whose red hair and blue-green eyes closely resembled those of her adoring father, experienced her first real change at the age of two, when the family moved to the new mansion Hugh Bell had built in the town of Redcar, overlooking the North Sea. Known as Red Barns, the family estate stretched out over several acres and contained numerous gardens (including one for Gertrude), a racquet court, a bicycle house, a pond, and stables. The nursery occupied a separate wing of the house, but Gertrude could wander freely through the mansion, exploring its 14 bedrooms, its greenhouses, and the huge kitchen. She also went for walks along the coastline with her nanny.

In early 1871, Gertrude Bell's life changed in a more permanent and devastating way. Mary Bell suffered severe complications following the birth of a baby boy, Maurice. Two-year-old Gertrude Bell lost her beloved mother.

Gertrude's father became her constant companion, and she followed him everywhere, sharing his interests in horseback riding, in exploring the countryside, and in gardening. As a young girl, she wrote letters to her father, full of details of her gardens. In her earliest surviving letter, Gertrude wrote to her father on July 12, 1874, only two days before her sixth birthday:

> . . . . The duck is sitting on five eggs, she is going to have some young ones. The garden is growing very well. Pilcher has done that bed, it looks very pretty. Yesterday it was wet after dinner but it brightened up in the evening and we were able to go out for a few minutes to gather poppy a [sic] nosegay we had a beautiful rose in it, I think that it was from my garden. . . [10]

Like most wealthy young women, Gertrude was taught German and French, literature, art, fancy needlework, painting, and music. She learned how to swim, how to play tennis, and how to ride horses.

Gertrude, however, had inherited her grandfather's and father's intellect and ambition. She had a healthy mix of curiosity about the world, interest in new ideas, and the courage to test herself. She would not be content simply to become a proper young lady.

A STEPMOTHER

When Gertrude was eight years old, her father remarried. His new wife was the 24-year-old playwright Florence Olliffe. Florence had grown up in France and was the daughter of the well-known physician Sir Joseph Olliffe. She had spent her youth surrounded by prominent people, including Henry James and Charles Dickens. Hugh Bell was quickly entranced by her sophistication and elegance.

The wedding took place in London on August 10, 1876. Gertrude and her younger brother were not invited. The day before the ceremony, Gertrude wrote, "My dear Miss Olliffe I write this letter for you to have on your wedding day to send you and Papa our best love and many kisses."[11] A few days later, Gertrude began her letter to Florence with "My dear Mother," and noted somewhat poignantly, "I could not write to you before because I did not know the address. Maurice and I send our love and kisses to you and Papa. From your loving child Gertrude."[12]

From these letters it is clear that Gertrude desperately wanted to please her stepmother. Her stepmother, in turn, sent her gifts, including a locket and a doll. When Florence and Hugh returned from their honeymoon in America, the new family settled at Red Barns.

The couple traveled frequently, particularly to London, where Florence had many friends and frequently went for the staging of her plays. When they were at Red Barns, Florence spent much time reading to and with Gertrude. A particular favorite was the *Arabian Nights*.

Not all went as smoothly. Gertrude was an energetic, high-spirited little girl who had been allowed to run freely through the gardens and house, but her new stepmother was a perfectionist who brought her own ideas and thoughts on raising children to the marriage. Even in later years, traces of the conflict between the two were evident. In the two-volume *Letters of Gertrude Bell,* which Florence selected and edited, she noted critically:

> Gertrude never entirely mastered the art of spelling, and all her life long there were certain words in her letters that were always spelt wrong. She always wrote "siezed," "excercise," "exhorbitant." Sometimes "priviledge." [13]

As Gertrude grew older, and Florence and Hugh had their own children—Elsa, Molly, and Hugo—her father and step-mother began to search for the best way to channel her energy and feed her curious mind. Most girls of Gertrude's class and age were taught at home, but her parents were interested in a more progressive education and decided to send her to London, to the girls' school Queen's College, when she was 15 years old.

It was a dramatic change for Gertrude. She excelled in the class work, earning excellent grades in history, grammar, geography, French, and American history. She did not like life in London, missing the country and the much more relaxed rules of home. She wrote long letters home, describing everything that she saw and did.

Even from a distance, Florence continued to oversee Gertrude's education, insisting that she take piano lessons (which Gertrude hated) and correcting the grammar in her letters. Florence also made sure that Gertrude received regular deliveries of fresh flowers. When she was in London, she introduced Gertrude to many of her prominent friends.

Most young women of Gertrude's age and class were prepared for their "coming-out"; at the age of 17, they would be presented at court and introduced to society. For three years, they attended parties, teas, and balls with the ultimate goal of finding a suitable husband. Gertrude had other ideas.

Her enthusiasm for history had impressed the history teacher at Queen's College, Mr. Cramb. He made a radical suggestion that she attend Oxford University to continue her studies. Gertrude tentatively approached Hugh and Florence with the proposal, and they ultimately gave their consent.

A UNIVERSITY EDUCATION

In 1886, when Gertrude Bell first began classes at Oxford, she was one of only a few women on the prestigious campus. It had been only seven years since the university, which had trained the best and brightest minds in Great Britain since the twelfth century, had begun admitting female students, and the policy still had many fierce opponents. Just a short time before Gertrude's arrival, Dean John Burgon had offered female students this discouraging message, "Inferior to us God made you and inferior to the end of time you will remain." [14]

Indeed, the professors and male students were so uncomfortable with the presence of Gertrude and the few other women in their classrooms that extraordinary limitations were placed on them. In her first history class, Gertrude and the only other female student were led past the rows of tables and chairs designated for the 200 male students and escorted up to the platform from which the professor lectured. There, two separate seats had been placed for them, carefully segregated and in full view of the male students. In another history course, Gertrude was amused when the professor forced the female students to sit with their backs to him.

The clear distinction between male and female students did not bother Gertrude. A friend at Oxford, Janet Hogarth, later described the collegiate Gertrude as a ". . . vivid, rather untidy, auburn-haired girl" who

> took our hearts by storm with her brilliant talk and her youthful confidence in her self and her belongings. . . . She threw herself with untiring energy into every phase

of college life, she swam, she rowed, she played tennis, and hockey, she acted, she danced, she spoke in debates; she kept up with modern literature, and told us tales of modern authors, most of whom were her childhood's friends.[15]

Gradually, Gertrude lost some of the "untidiness" that marked her earliest appearance at Oxford. As her social life expanded to include chaperoned dates for skating and tea, she asked her stepmother for advice on fashion. Gertrude, however, was also studious and hard working, determined to prove herself the intellectual equal—or superior—of any student at Oxford.

By the end of two years—one year ahead of schedule— Gertrude was ready for her final examinations. The written examinations came first; Gertrude found them "delightful" and completed them so quickly that she had time for tennis and tea afterward.[16] The oral exams were much more difficult. Because these formally marked the end of a student's time at the university, parents frequently attended, sitting behind their children as they responded to questions from their professors. Florence and Hugh followed this tradition, and Florence later remembered seeing Gertrude "showing no trace of nervousness, sitting very upright at a table, beneath which her slender feet in neat brown shoes were crossed."[17]

The first questions came from S. R. Gardiner, a professor of history and a leading scholar on the reigns of King James I and King Charles I. When he asked Gertrude about Charles I, she boldly responded, "I am afraid I must differ from your estimate of Charles I," a comment that so horrified Gardiner that he immediately handed off the questioning to the professor seated next to him.[18] Gertrude answered several other questions until a professor asked her about a town in Germany, which he described as being on the left bank of the Rhine. Gertrude responded, "I am sorry, but it is on the right.

I know, I have been there." [19] Her boldness drew an audible gasp from those in the room.

Fortunately, her academic success was not hampered by this boldness. She had worked hard, and her performance earned her the highest mark in Modern History. She was the first woman to earn this distinction, and it was noted with an announcement in the *Times*.

Gertrude Bell was 20 years old. She was a celebrated student and the daughter of a leading industrialist. She was well educated and wealthy, she had a wide circle of friends, and she had spent time with many of the most prominent people in England. She was, in fact, lacking only one important thing: a husband.

A TRIP TO ROMANIA

While at Oxford, Gertrude had frequently spent time with her cousin by marriage, Billy Lascelles. His mother was Florence's sister, and the two women were soon in deep discussion about how best to make the highly educated and opinionated Gertrude more marriageable. The women decided that she needed to "get rid of her Oxfordy manner." [20]

Gertrude's stepaunt, Lady Mary Lascelles, suggested a trip. Lady Lascelles' husband, Sir Frank Lascelles, was serving as the British minister to Romania, and it was decided that a winter spent at the British Embassy in the cosmopolitan city of Bucharest would be just the thing to erase some of Gertrude's "Oxfordy manner."

In December 1888, Gertrude and her father traveled to Paris where they met Billy Lascelles. Billy then escorted Gertrude to Bucharest—her first trip without a chaperone. Bucharest was a city of glamorous and wealthy people; as a guest of the British Embassy, Gertrude soon found herself the subject of numerous invitations. In one letter, Gertrude noted:

> Last Sunday which was their first of January, there was a big ball at the palace which was very good fun. I was

presented to the King and Queen but the King was so like every other officer that I never could remember who he was and only merciful providence prevented me from giving him a friendly little nod several times during the evening under the impression that he was one of my numerous acquaintance whom I had not yet seen. Billy and I waltzed over his toes once. "Ware King"—whispered Billy, but it was too late. However he didn't seem to mind. I was taken down to supper by a tall befezed Turk—the Turkish military attaché I think he was. I saw he looked rather depressed and he presently confided to me the cause of his grief; it was very serious; his waistband was too tight and he could not eat any supper! So he stood gloomily by and helped me to all kinds of excellent dishes while I was consumed with a desire to laugh.[21]

Gertrude was happy with the social whirl, enjoying the glamorous surroundings without being overly impressed by any of the people she met. She enjoyed the company of many diplomats and foreign dignitaries. During this period she met Valentine Chirol (nicknamed Domnul, the Romanian word for "gentleman"), a friend of the Lascelleses who was serving as foreign correspondent for the *Times*. Chirol spoke numerous languages and had traveled throughout Europe and the East. He was a source of information, both for the British government and for Gertrude, and would become one of her lifelong friends.

In late April 1889, the Lascelleses decided to take Gertrude to Constantinople, the capital of the Ottoman Empire. The mighty Ottoman Empire had once stretched from Iraq to Austria and contained Turkey, Mesopotamia, Egypt, Arabia, Syria, Persia (now Iran), Hungary, Bulgaria, Romania, Albania, Bosnia, Herzegovina, Serbia, and Greece within its borders. Wars and corruption had progressively weakened the empire, and gradually bits of it had slipped away.

The politics of the Ottoman Empire would one day matter deeply to Gertrude, but on this first visit to the East, she focused only on the exotic beauty of this new world. The minarets sparkling in the sun, the rich colors of the bazaars, and the Turkish food and strong Turkish coffee all entranced her; for a brief period of time, she even believed herself in love with Billy, who shared this adventure with her. She was 20 years old. Most young women her age were already married, and as she traveled with Billy back to London on the Orient Express, the romance of all she had seen made her believe that the romance was because of Billy rather than the environment.

Back in London, however, as they spent time together in more familiar surroundings, it soon became clear to Gertrude that Billy was not the right man for her. Gertrude had been spoiled by a lifetime surrounded by intelligent, adventurous men.[22] Billy could not meet this high standard, and the romance soon cooled.

AN UNMARRIED WOMAN

The next few years were difficult for Gertrude. She was in her 20s now, several years older than many of the young women just coming out, and she was more intelligent, better educated, and better traveled than most of the men to whom she was introduced. She continued to attend parties and balls, escorted by her stepmother or aunt. She shuttled back and forth between Red Barns and London, spending time in the city during the social season of parties and returning to the family home at Red Barns for the fall and winter months. There, she kept busy tutoring her young half sisters, helping manage the household, and doing some social work among the wives of the workers at the Bell Brothers' factories.

By early 1892, Gertrude had despaired of finding a man strong enough and intelligent enough to be her husband. She was focusing more on adding to her knowledge of the East. By February 1892, she was trying to find someone to give her lessons in Persian. The land now known as Iran had fascinated her for some time, and the lessons were an indication that she was preparing for another trip.

The opportunity came in early 1892. Sir Frank Lascelles had been appointed British minister to Persia's capital, Tehran, and Lady Mary invited Gertrude to travel there with her. Gertrude, her aunt, and her cousin Florence boarded the Orient Express in Paris and traveled to Constantinople. There, they caught a boat, arriving in Tehran on May 7, 1892.

In a letter to her cousin Horace Marshall dated June 18, 1892, Gertrude indicated the transformation that had begun:

> Are we the same people I wonder when all our surroundings, associations, acquaintances are changed? . . . How big the world is, how big and how wonderful. It comes to me as ridiculously presumptuous that I should dare to carry my little personality half across it and boldly attempt to measure with it things for which it has no table of measurements that can possibly apply.[23]

3

The Colors
of the East

The beauty Gertrude Bell found in Tehran was particularly striking after her long and dusty journey from Constantinople. "Oh the desert round Teheran!" Bell wrote to her cousin, "miles and miles of it with nothing, *nothing* growing; ringed in with bleak bare mountains snow crowned and furrowed with the deep courses of torrents."[24]

In Tehran, however, there were colors everywhere. The embassy walls were covered with roses—yellow, white, red, and purple. It was an exotic world, as Bell noted:

> . . . the houses which we heard of in fairy tales when we were little: inlaid with tiny slabs of looking-glass in lovely patterns, blue tiled, carpeted, echoing with the sound of running water and fountains. Here sits the enchanted prince, solemn, dignified, clothed in long robes. He comes down to meet you as you enter, his house is yours, his garden is yours, better still his tea and fruit are yours.[25]

The embassy was as fine as any prince's home, outfitted with servants in elegant uniforms, huge rooms for entertaining, and numerous bedrooms. Through it all drifted the perfume of the roses. One member of the embassy staff quickly made an impression on Bell: Henry Cadogan, the embassy's first secretary. Bell's letters home were full of her descriptions of ". . . Mr. Cadogan, tall and red and very thin, agreeable, intelligent, a great tennis player, a great billiard player . . . devoted to riding though he can't ride in the least, smart, clean, well dressed, looking upon us as his special property to be looked after and amused—I like him . . ."[26]

Cadogan, ten years older than Bell, was intelligent and well traveled. He spoke several languages, including Persian; was familiar with many of Bell's favorite authors; and was soon escorting her all around Tehran. Bell's letters to her stepmother noted that ". . . Mr. Cadogan is the real treasure; it is certainly unexpected and undeserved to have come all the way to Tehran and find someone so delightful at the end." [27]

When hot weather caused the temperatures to rise, the entire embassy staff relocated to the summer embassy in the hills of Gulahek. There, Bell spent her mornings reading Persian poetry (in the original language) while resting in a hammock next to a tiny stream or bathing in a tub scented with rosewater after a dusty horseback ride. She was also spending time with the charming Henry Cadogan, picnicking, reading poetry, taking walks, and playing tennis.

As the relationship became more serious, both Bell and Cadogan wrote letters to her father, requesting his permission to marry. There was one problem. Cadogan, although the grandson of the third Earl Cadogan, had not inherited any kind of money, and his salary as a low-level diplomat was not enough to support both himself and Bell. After several weeks, a response came from Bell's father. He was not in favor of the engagement and suggested instead that Bell come home to see if a separation would help, believing perhaps that the romance of Persia, as much as the charms of Mr. Cadogan, had contributed to his daughter's state of mind.

Bell was 24 years old and Henry Cadogan was 33 years old, but they both believed in the codes and behavior of their time. They did not ignore Henry Bell's suggestion; instead, they decided to wait and hope that perhaps a promotion might bring more income to Cadogan and make him a more attractive suitor in Henry Bell's eyes.

Bell was obedient but heartbroken. She wrote to her stepmother:

> I care more than I can say, and I'm not afraid of being poor or even of having to wait, though waiting is harder than I thought it would be at first. For one doesn't

realize at first how one will long for the constant com-
panionship and the blessed security of being married,
but now that I am going away I realise it wildly . . . our
position is very difficult and we are very unhappy.[28]

Bell began making arrangements to return to England,
spending less time with Cadogan to honor her father's
wishes but hoping that circumstances would soon reunite
them. As she prepared to leave Persia, she again wrote to
her stepmother:

> Everything I think and write brings us back to things we
> have spoken of together, sentences of his that come
> flashing like sharp swords; you see for the last three
> months nothing I have done or thought has not had
> him in it, the essence of it all. . . . You must not think for
> a moment that if I could choose I would not have it all
> over again, impatience and pain and the going which is
> yet to come. It is worth it all, more than worth it. Some
> people live all their lives and never have this wonderful
> thing; at least I have known it and seen life's possibili-
> ties suddenly open in front of me—only one may cry
> just a little when one has to turn away and take up the
> old narrow life again.[29]

Bell was escorted home by her cousin, Gerald Lascelles.
It was a long and bleak trip, and although Bell tried to
remain hopeful, her mood did not improve when she arrived
in London in chilly late October.

PERSIAN PICTURES

To help preserve her memories of Persia, Bell began writing,
noting her experiences of traveling in the East for a book that
would eventually become *Persian Pictures*. She wrote of
Tehran, of the rich colors of the bazaars, and of the strong

perfumes of the gardens. She wrote of the warm hospitality of the people and the desolate emptiness of the desert.

All of her memories were entangled with memories of Cadogan, and each day, as she sat down to write, she remembered another conversation, another experience they had shared. For eight months, she worked on the book. Then, in August 1893, she received a telegram from Tehran. The message was brief: Henry Cadogan had been trout fishing, and had fallen into the icy waters of the River Lar. The chill had brought on a case of pneumonia. Cadogan was dead.[30]

For several months, Bell was grief stricken. The manuscript pages of *Persian Pictures* were a painful reminder of what she had lost. Eventually, under some pressure from her father and stepmother, she reluctantly agreed to allow the manuscript to be published. The book was published in the spring of 1894, at first anonymously. Only later was it republished under Gertrude Bell's name.

Bell longed to travel, but she felt that another trip to the East would be too painful. For the next five years, she traveled around Europe, visiting friends and relatives. At the same time, she reread many of the poems she and Cadogan had read together, struck now more by the tragic tones in the poetry that seemed, in retrospect, so clear. She decided to work on a translation of the poems of the Persian writer Hafiz.

For two years, Bell concentrated on translating the complex stanzas of Hafiz into English, and in 1897, *Poems from the Divan of Hafiz* was published to glowing reviews. A century later, the translation was still highly acclaimed, with one scholar stating, "Though some twenty hands have put Hafiz into English, her rendering remains the best!"[31]

The emotion of the Persian poetry was close to Bell's own heart, contributing to her understanding of the true meaning of the poems. Her translation of the poem "To Hafiz of Shiraz" begins:

Thus said the Poet: "When Death comes to you,
All ye whose life-sand through the hour-glass slips,
He lays two fingers on your ears, and two
Upon your eyes he lays, one on your lips,
Whispering: Silence." Although deaf thine ear,
Thine eye, my Hafiz, suffer Time's eclipse,
The songs thou sangest still all men may hear.

Songs of dead laughter, songs of love once hot,
Songs of a cup once flushed rose-red with wine,
Songs of a rose whose beauty is forgot,
A nightingale that piped hushed lays divine:
And still a graver music runs beneath
The tender love notes of those songs of thine,
Oh, Seeker of the keys of Life and Death![32]

RUNNING FROM SORROW

Bell could not bear to remain still and settled. Life in England was full of reminders that, now in her late 20s, she had become an "old maid." It was her younger half-sisters who were dressing up for balls and parties. Gertrude traveled to Switzerland and Italy. She went with her father to Algeria, back to Switzerland, and then to Germany.

In each location, she took lessons to learn the native language. She perfected her German and learned Italian. She also began taking lessons in Arabic and soon was able to read the Koran and *Arabian Nights* in the original language.

By 1897, new grief weighed on Bell. In April, her aunt, Mary Lascelles, who had taken her to Romania and then to Persia, died. Next came the death of a close friend from Oxford who had died following complications from childbirth.

The sadness was overwhelming, and Bell felt that she had to escape, at least temporarily. On December 29, 1987, she and her brother, Maurice, set sail on a package trip that would take them around the world. It was more of a luxury cruise than the kind of exotic travel Gertrude would later undertake, but she felt at peace as the boat sailed across the Atlantic. She traveled to Jamaica, Guatemala, and San Francisco, and then on to Tokyo and Hong Kong. Her journey ended with a stop in the French Alps, where she discovered a new love: mountain climbing.

She returned to London in June 1898 and focused once more on perfecting her understanding of Arabic and Persian, but she was restless. In the spring of 1899, Bell traveled to northern Italy and then, with her father, to Greece. In Greece, she met David Hogarth, the brother of her friend from Oxford, Janet Hogarth. Hogarth was an archeologist who was excavating the 6,000-year-old city of Melos, and Bell was fascinated by the work. In a letter home she noted, "He took us from stone to stone and built up a wonderful chain of evidence with extraordinary ingenuity until we saw the Athens of 600 B.C. I never saw anything better done."[33]

Bell then traveled alone through Switzerland to the French Alps. She had decided to test herself by climbing the 13,081-foot-high Grand Pic de la Meije. It was an ambitious project, tackled only by the most experienced climbers. At one point, Bell and her guides encountered a blizzard and were forced to cling to a narrow ledge for several hours. After a grueling climb, Bell successfully reached the top, an experience that gave her the confidence to tackle future adventures. As she wrote to her father once she had completed the climb, "I think if I had known exactly what was before me I should not have faced it, but fortunately did not, and I look back on it with unmixed satisfaction—and forward to other things with no further apprehension. . ."[34]

Bell returned home. At the age of 31, she was better traveled, better educated, and more fluent in more languages than nearly every person she met. She was also lonely and restless. She found real happiness in only one place—the Middle East—so she decided to return there. In November

1899, she set out on another journey. This time her destination was Jerusalem.

PILGRIMAGE TO THE DESERT

Bell traveled to Jerusalem to improve her Arabic, to spend time in a region that she loved, and also to visit with Friedrich Rosen and his family. The Rosens were friends of the Bells, and Friedrich Rosen was serving as the German consulate in Jerusalem. Gertrude's hotel was only a short distance from the consulate, and she spent time each day visiting with the Rosens and studying Arabic.

The language eluded her. She had mastered the basics when still in England, but even after spending five hours a day in study, she still found it difficult:

> I either have a lesson or work alone every morning for 4 hours—the lesson only lasts 1-1/2 hours. I have 3 morning and 3 afternoon lessons a week. I am just beginning to understand a little of what I hear and to say simple things to the servants, but I find it awfully difficult.[35]

Bell went for long rides, observing the Christian, Jewish, and Muslim pilgrims visiting the sites holy to their faiths. She rode to the Dead Sea. Finally, she planned a more ambitious journey—one that would take her into the desert alone. She hired some guides and a cook and set out in March 1900, sending her team on ahead so that she could enjoy the ride out of Jerusalem without distractions.

She passed groups of tourists and moved on to the Jordan River, where she learned that her tents still had not arrived. She met her guide, Tarif, and they decided to stay in Jericho for the night before setting out again early the next day. She was overwhelmed by the wilderness at the edge of the desert: "sheets and sheets of varied and exquisite colour—purple, white, yellow, and the brightest blue."[36] Although Bell recognized a few of the plants, most of them were new to her.

Bell rode sidesaddle, wearing a divided skirt. It was a novelty to see a Western woman traveling alone in the desert, and she attracted attention. Shortly after making camp on their second day in the desert, the group was surrounded by a group of Arab women who sold them a hen and some sour milk, a kind of yogurt called *laban*. Later, Bell dined on a delicious meal of soup made from rice and olive oil, Irish stew, and raisins.

On the third day, Bell was forced to practice a little diplomacy. She wanted to continue her journey into the desert, but she needed permission from the Turkish authorities in charge of the region. She sent a message, and soon, a tall, middle-aged Turkish official appeared. Bell offered him cigarettes and coffee. Gradually, using her best manners and conversational skills, she discovered that the official hoped to be photographed with his soldiers. Bell quickly offered to take the photograph and provide him with copies, at which point he responded that he would happily provide her with a soldier to escort her on the next phase of her journey.

On the following day, the promised escort, a handsome, cheerful Circassian riding a white horse, appeared. The travelers soon reached the ruins of Mashetta, a Persian palace dating back to the seventh century. "The beauty of it all was quite past words," Bell wrote. "It's a thing one will never forget as long as one lives."[37]

For several days, rising at dawn, Bell explored the region. She saw what was rumored to be the tomb of Noah; she bathed in streams. She rode to the top of Mount Hor, where she found magnificent cliffs, colored red, yellow, blue, and white. She explored the Roman ruins of the city of Petra—the hidden city that had once served as the capital of the Nabateans and had played an important role in desert trade but had, over the centuries, been buried in the desert sand.

Bell needed special permission from the Turkish authorities to make the two-day journey to Petra; waiting for it proved worth the effort. The ruins were marked by an entranceway of red sandstone rocks that arched nearly 100 feet high and a temple carved from pink rock. Bell spent the night camping in the middle of Petra's hundreds of tombs, some rising three stories high.

On the return journey, she searched for ancient milestones left by the Romans when they had conquered the region. Bell wrote of the lack of water at points along the journey and of the times when food was scarce, but in all of her letters it is clear that she was not complaining. She was happy sitting by the flickering light of the campfire, sunburned from a day spent in the hot sun. By April 9, back in Jerusalem, she wrote to her stepsister:

> The more you see, the more everything falls into a kind
> of rough and ready perspective, and when you come to
> a new thing, you haven't so much difficulty in placing it
> and fitting it into the rest. I'm awfully glad you love the
> beginnings of things—so do I, most thoroughly, and
> unless one does, I don't believe one can get as much
> pleasure out of the ends.[38]

Bell herself was at a kind of beginning. She had discovered a new strength in herself during those days on horseback and those nights by the campfire. She was soon planning another journey, this time deeper into uncharted territory, to see the land of the Druze.

A DANGEROUS ROAD

In mid-April 1900, accompanied by the Rosens, Bell left Jerusalem. Witnessing Bell's discomfort on the long journey, Friedrich Rosen removed the sidesaddle from her horse and showed her how to ride with a man's saddle instead. By the time she left the Rosens, north of Jerusalem, she had mastered the art of riding more comfortably and was rejoicing at the fact that, "Till I speak the people always think I'm a man and address me as Effendim! You mustn't think I haven't got a most elegant and decent divided skirt, however, but as all men wear skirts of sorts too, that doesn't serve to distinguish me."[39] Her appearance was further disguised by a big white *keffieh* scarf wound around her hat and face, which allowed only her eyes to peek through, and a coat that protected her from the wind and sun.

Bell also rejoiced in the comfort of once more living in tents, sipping a cup of tea by the campfire, and enjoying the sight of Mount Hermon rising like "a white cloud hanging in mid air."[40] Her goal was to reach the little-explored terrain of the Druze, a Muslim sect that was battling the Ottoman Turks and had gained a reputation as fierce warriors. At the time, the Druze controlled territory that touched upon parts of Lebanon, southern Syria, and the area known as Galilee. Bell would be one of the few westerners to set foot in their territory. Once again, the expedition could not proceed without the permission of the Turkish authorities.

Bell arranged a meeting with the Turkish administrator in Bosrah, near the Druze border. When he learned that she was traveling to Damascus, he complimented her for choosing this destination and then indicated the best western road to take, where she might find some beautiful ruins. Bell thanked him for the suggestion and promised to travel to the ruins but then said that she first wished to travel east to visit Salakhad. "There is nothing there at all," the official responded firmly, "and the road is very dangerous. It cannot happen."

"It must happen," Bell replied firmly, adding, "English women are never afraid. I wish to look upon the ruins."[41] Bell told the official that she would be staying in Basra for the night and then explored the city, deciding that if she were not given official permission, she would still attempt the journey.

She would leave early in the morning to get a head start and prevent the Turks—who feared entering Druze territory—from following her.

She went into her tent early, reading by candlelight until she heard voices outside. She quickly blew out the light and pretended to be asleep, listening to her servant speaking to a Turkish official who requested that she inform the authorities before going anywhere. Bell decided to change her plans and got up at two in the morning. She packed in the cold light of the stars and within an hour was on her way, determined to travel farther north, to Areh, where she believed a powerful Druze sheikh, who might be able to offer her protection, lived. She and her team quietly slipped out of town, heading into Druze territory.

Bell traveled into the mountains and was quickly astonished at the hospitality she found. She was a curiosity, and wherever she went, she was surrounded by men who wanted to shake her hand or—in one surprising instance—kiss her cheeks. One offered his services as a guide and led her into Areh.

At Areh, she was warmly welcomed by the villagers, who invited her for coffee. The men walked with her, hand-in-hand with their little fingers linked, as was the Druze style, and when they learned she was English, she was greeted like a hero. They led her to the local Druze chief, a handsome, middle-aged man who was seated in a circle with six or seven other men, eating from a large plate. Bell was welcomed into the circle, and soon she too was eating the *laban*, beans, and meat, using thin slices of bread for utensils. "I should liked to have eaten much more of it," Bell noted, "but the Beg [chief] had finished and I was afraid it wouldn't be polite." [42]

When the plate had been removed, Bell was invited to sit with the head Druze on a cushion on the floor and tell him of her travels. She took his photograph, posing him on his verandah, and eventually he agreed to her request for an escort. She traveled on, suffering the hot days and cold nights and feeling grateful that she had brought her winter clothes with her. She was also grateful for her strong stomach. She was constantly being offered a wide range of foods at all times of the day and night and was able to eat and enjoy nearly everything.

By May 11, 1900, she had left the Druze territory and entered Damascus. It was strange to come out of the desert, following the caravans of camels laden with goods, and into the bright colors of the bazaar. At the German consulate, she found a box of clothes that she had sent on from Jerusalem and a packet of letters from her family. Her family had also wired her more money, so she was able to hire a cook, a guide, and three Kurdish soldiers for yet another journey—to the town of Jarad and on into the desert.

The nights were bitterly cold, the days terribly hot. She was far from the roads normally traveled by tourists, and her Arabic was getting better. She rode to Palmyra, marveling at "the mass of columns, ranged into long avenues, grouped into temples, lying broken on the sand or pointing one long solitary finger to Heaven." She spent two days exploring the region, drinking water from the sulfur-laced springs and watching the dust clouds rise up from the desert before returning to Damascus.

Finally, she traveled to Beirut and then to Jaffa, where she caught a boat for England. "But you know, dearest Father," she wrote, "I shall be back here before long! One doesn't keep away from the East when one has got into it this far."[44]

4

The Voice
of the Wind

Despite what she had written in the letter to her father, Gertrude Bell stayed in Europe for nearly two years. She spent time in Yorkshire with her family, traveled to London to meet with friends, and played tennis and golf, always keeping herself busy. In August 1900, she traveled to Switzerland, climbing the Alpine peaks of Chamonix and Mer de Glacé before bad weather prevented her from attempting any other climbs.

Bell returned to Switzerland a year later. She was 33 years old, and she was determined to climb 9,130-feet-high Mount Engelhorn. On September 6, 1901, she set out before dawn with two guides. It was a treacherous climb, made worse by rain and sleet. Bell wanted to attempt the climb from either the north or south side—routes that had never before been taken. Soon, the rain was pouring down so heavily that it soaked the climbers' necks and sleeves, and even the insides of their boots. They abandoned the climb and returned the next day. This time, they reached a higher point, but the rock was sheer, with few crevices or ledges from which to get a handgrip. After a time, they reached a very steep point just below an overhang. None of the climbers was tall enough to reach it, so they were forced to stand on each other's shoulders. Bell climbed on top of one of her guides; another balanced himself on her shoulders. The guide on Bell's shoulders called out, "I don't feel at all safe—if you move we are all killed," but Bell (despite feeling as if she were slipping) calmly replied, "All right, I can stand here for a week." [45] Eventually, he was able to pull himself up onto the ledge, and the others followed. They reached the top of Engelhorn, spending the night in a shepherd's hayloft before heading for home. By the time she returned to England, Bell had climbed eight additional mountain peaks.

NEW ADVENTURES

At the beginning of 1902, Gertrude once more journeyed to the East, traveling at first with her father and half brother, Hugo, to Algeria and Naples. From Naples, she traveled alone to Malta to spend some time at an archeological dig. From Malta, she traveled to Haifa, hiring two sheikhs to help her improve her Persian and Arabic. She was excited to discover that stories of her travels and adventures preceded her, and on March 30, she wrote to her father: "I am much entertained to find that I am a Person in this country— they all think I was a Person! and one of the first questions everyone seems to ask everyone else is 'Have you ever met Miss Gertrude Bell?'"[46]

Bell studied in the mornings; in the afternoons, she rode out to explore different archeological sites, photographing the ruins and the people she saw. She struggled with Arabic, finding Persian much easier. At the end of May, she returned to England, spending a month there before traveling once more to Switzerland.

This time, accompanied by two guides, she climbed the peak of the Wellhorn, 10,485 feet high. Next, she targeted the Finsteraarhorn glacier, whose face rose 3,000 feet high. It was a particularly dangerous choice, but Bell was determined to challenge herself. The climbers encountered storm clouds, bitter temperatures, snow, lightning, and thunder; the steepness of the rock face made finding shelter practically impossible. The ropes were ice-covered and difficult to handle; avalanches constantly threatened. It became so dangerous that they were forced to turn back, finding the conditions every bit as treacherous as they tried to make their way back down the mountain's steep face. At one point, they were forced to huddle together for 16 hours, with only a few scraps of food and a few sips of brandy to sustain them, until the weather cleared enough for them to proceed. Bell wrote of the experience, ". . . I think that when things are as bad as ever they can be you cease to mind them much. You set your teeth and battle with the fates. . ."[47]

After Bell's death, an article praising her mountaineering skills was published in the *Alpine Journal*:

Everything that she undertook, physical or mental, was accomplished so superlatively well, that it would indeed have been strange if she had not shone on a mountain as she did in the hunting-field or in the desert. Her strength, incredible in that slim frame, her endurance, above all her courage, were so great that even to this day her guide . . . speaks with an admiration of her that amounts to veneration. He told the writer, some years ago, that of all the amateurs, men or women, that he had travelled with, he had seen but very few to surpass her in technical skill and none to equal her in coolness, bravery and judgment. [48]

AROUND THE WORLD

Late in 1902, Gertrude and Hugo Bell set out on a trip that would take them around the world. Hugo was considering a career in the church; they spent much of the journey arguing about this—Hugo for and Gertrude against. Their first stop was India, where a celebration was taking place to mark the coronation of King Edward VII of England. India was an important part of the British Empire, often described as the "jewel in the crown." Thus, in ascending to the throne of England, Edward VII was also becoming ruler of India.

The festivities drew many of the most important diplomats and dignitaries from Great Britain, and Gertrude found many old friends in India, including Domnul Chirol. Chirol introduced her to members of the Indian civil service, the British administrators who ruled the colony. One in particular proved to be an important contact: the British consul in

Muscat, Percy Cox. They talked of local and regional politics, and Cox and Chirol discussed the conflict brewing between Ibn Saud and Ibn Rashid, the two powerful clan leaders who controlled most of Arabia.

Bell and her brother then traveled further east, stopping in Singapore, Shanghai, Seoul, and Tokyo. They continued across the Pacific to Vancouver, where Bell again tested her climbing skills on several peaks of the Rocky Mountains in the lovely setting of Lake Louise. Accompanied by a guide, she scaled Mount Stephen, giving herself a black eye when she accidentally bumped her cheek against her ice ax. She found the setting spectacular and was astonished to encounter three Swiss guides who knew her from earlier climbs in Switzerland. They climbed several peaks together before Bell continued her travels across the United States. Bell was underwhelmed by the "filth of the streets, the noise, the ugliness" of Chicago. [49] She and Hugo quickly passed on to Niagara Falls and Boston before departing for England.

By July 1903, Bell was back in England. She helped her stepsister plan her wedding, climbed mountains in Switzerland, and then decided to study architecture and ancient civilizations in preparation for another trip to the East. She traveled to Paris to work with Salomon Reinach, a scholar of Middle Eastern culture, and pored over French texts on artifacts and ancient civilizations.

Bell had hoped to make a trip to Arabia to explore the unknown desert there and meet with Ibn Rashid and Ibn Saud, but her contacts there suggested that it was still too dangerous. Instead, she began plans for a different trip, one that would take her from Jerusalem into Syria. The journey would take her back over some of the terrain she had crossed several years earlier, into the territory of the Druze. She wanted to gather material for a book that would provide English readers with a sense of the East that she loved—its archeology, its people, its culture.

THE DESERT AND THE SOWN

In *The Desert and the Sown*, Gertrude Bell's account of her travels into Syria, she wrote memorably of the impulse that carried her into unknown territory:

> The voice of the wind shall be heard instead of the persuasive voices of counsellors, the touch of the rain and the prick of the frost shall be spurs sharper than praise or blame, and necessity shall speak with an authority unknown to that borrowed wisdom which men obey or discard at will. So you leave the sheltered close, and, like the man in the fairy story, you feel the bands break that were riveted about your heart as you enter the path that stretches across the rounded shoulder of the earth.[50]

She left England in January 1905. From Beirut, she wrote to her father:

> I'm deep in the gossip of the East! It's so enjoyable. I thought to-day when I was strolling through the bazaars buying various odds and ends what a pleasure it was to be in the East almost as part of it, to know it all as I know Syria now, to be able to tell from the accent and the dress of the people where they come from and exchange the proper greeting as one passes.[51]

In Beirut, she purchased some of the supplies she would need for her journey and arranged for horses and mules and three guides. Then she traveled to Jerusalem, where she completed her preparations and hired a cook. Later, an Arab guide would also join the party.

Bell left at dawn on the stormy morning of February 5, the mules carrying her two tents, food and water, and two trunks. She traveled east, heading for the Jordan valley, which she described as having "an aspect of inhumanity that is almost evil."[52] Rain fell briefly, adding to the somber atmosphere and then leaving the road muddy and difficult for the mules to travel. The group passed on to the Jordan Bridge, "the most inspiring piece of architecture in the world, since it is the Gate of the Desert."[53]

Bell was thrilled to camp once more under the stars. For the 37-year-old Englishwoman, there were few pleasures that could match the joy she felt sitting next to the fire and listening to Arabic. She passed through the large city of Salt, riding through its rich fields of grape vines and apricot trees, and then through the empty treeless valleys east of Jordan. She saw in the land an image from the poetry of *The Rubáiyát of Omar Khayyám*, inspiring the title of her book: "The strip of herbage strown that just divides the desert from the sown."[54]

Bell photographed the ruins of ancient civilizations as she traveled into the desert. The photographs would ultimately be used to illustrate her book. She began to understand more fully the richness of the desert:

> The Arabs do not speak of desert or wilderness as we do. Why should they? To them it is neither desert nor wilderness, but a land of which they know every feature, a mother country whose smallest product has a use sufficient for their needs.[55]

Bell also described and photographed the people she encountered. She offered detailed and thoughtful observations of the politics of the region and of the tenuous relationships between the Ottoman authorities and the people they ruled.

On one occasion, Bell witnessed a group of young Druze warriors—men and boys—preparing for battle, singing—or really shouting—a terrifying martial song. Amazingly, she was invited to join their circle as they prepared themselves for war. One warrior declared to her as he raised his sword above his head, "Lady! The English and the Druze are one," to which she quickly responded, "Thank God! We, too, are a fighting race."[56]

She copied the inscriptions from ancient ruins, hoping that they would prove of interest to archeologists. Then she passed on into Syria.

During these travels, Bell was beginning to gain a greater appreciation for the stark differences between the peoples loosely united under Ottoman rule. She noted:

> We in Europe, who speak of Turkey as though it were a homogeneous empire, might as well when we speak of England intend the word to include India, the Shan States, Hongkong and Uganda. In the sense of a land inhabited mainly by Turks there is not such a country as Turkey. The parts of his dominions where the Turk is in a majority are few; generally his position is that of an alien governing, with a handful of soldiers and an empty purse, a mixed collection of subjects hostile to him and to each other.[57]

She traveled farther east, into Asia Minor, exploring and photographing ancient Roman and Byzantine ruins. The research she gathered would ultimately provide the material for several articles for archeological journals.

Gertrude closed *The Desert and the Sown* with the words of her guide Mikhail. As they neared the Syrian border, Mikhail remarked:

> Listen, oh lady, and I will make it clear to you. Men are short of vision, and they see but that for which they look. Some look for evil and they find evil; some look for good and it is good that they find, and moreover some are fortunate and these find always what they want. Praise be to God! To that number you belong. . . .

ACCOMPLISHED AUTHOR

Bell returned to England and quickly began gathering her notes into the book that would become *The Desert and the Sown*. She wanted to publish something more than a travel memoir—she wanted her book to have lasting value and to prove her reputation both as a traveler and a scholar. It was not until December 1906 that the manuscript was completed. Her father had moved into a large mansion at Rounton Grange, and as Bell wrote, she also enjoyed the lush Yorkshire gardens and the luxurious comfort of the estate after months spent camping under the stars.

When her book was published, it received glowing reviews. Reassured by the favorable response to her writing, Bell began to plan another trip to the East. This time she offered her services to William Ramsay, a noted archeologist who was planning to excavate church ruins in Turkey. In March 1907, Bell traveled to Asia Minor to meet Ramsay, suggesting that they collaborate both on the excavation and on a book about their discoveries. That book, reviewing the plans and measurements of the remains they discovered, was eventually published in 1909 and was titled *The Thousand and One Churches*.

On the way to meet Ramsay, Bell stopped at Konia to collect her mail and make the necessary travel arrangements with the British officials there. The British consul was a young soldier, a Major Charles (Richard) Doughty-Wylie. He was the nephew of the noted Arabian explorer Charles Doughty, and soon Bell had formed a friendship with Major Doughty-Wylie and his wife.

She continued working with Ramsay. The long hours of the dig did not quench Bell's enthusiasm. The team was too busy to cook, so they lived on eggs and rice and sour milk. They targeted unexplored areas in hopes of finding previously undocumented churches. Often they found nothing, and when they did find ruins, the work was painstaking, hot, and laborious. As the ruins were carefully uncovered, inscriptions and patterns were noted and the site was photographed. Through it all, Bell kept her sense of humor. On July 6, she wrote to her family:

> We are now going round to the north side of the mountain where I am told there are a million if not a billion churches—or something of the kind. I hope there may be one or two. I know how you are spending this Sunday [her stepsister was being married]—how I wish I were with you! I also wish so many flies were not spending Sunday with me.[59]

By August 9, she was back in London, meeting with friends and notables and discussing all that she had seen. She found a new passion—she went to the Royal Geographical Society for training in surveying and making astronomical observations, skills that she hoped would prove useful on her planned trip into Arabia.

5

The Romance
of the Desert

Early in 1909, Bell returned to the East, this time to travel from Syria into Mesopotamia, the region we now know as Iraq. She had initially hoped to travel to Arabia, but friends once again advised her that the trip was too dangerous. She wanted to write another book, similar to *The Desert and the Sown*, and decided to begin in Syria, at the site of some ancient Hittite ruins, before traveling on to Mesopotamia. The Hittites had ruled much of western Asia from 1400 to 1200 B.C., and their ruins were often a rich source of interesting, round sculptures and inscriptions in cuneiform.

Bell was accompanied by her servant, Fattuh, who helped arrange her supplies: tents, a folding bed, mosquito netting, a canvas bath, a canvas chair, rugs, table, pots and pans, a month's worth of food, linens, china, a tea set, and crystal and silver. There were seven animals to carry the baggage, 12 horses, one additional servant, three guides, and two soldiers.[60]

The border between Syria and Mesopotamia was marked by the Euphrates River, which she crossed in a narrow boat. David Hogarth had asked her to study several Hittite ruins in Mesopotamia that marked the remains of the ancient city of Carchemish.

Bell found much of the terrain around the river dull and the travel around it uninteresting. The river apparently flooded the terrain every two to three decades, effectively obliterating most traces of earlier civilizations. The days were hot, and dust was everywhere.

By mid-March, she had left the area around the Euphrates and crossed into the desert, sending some of her supplies ahead of her to Baghdad. On one of the early days of her journey, her team spent ten hours traveling without encountering another human being.

For nine days, she traveled across the desert, spotting a herd of gazelles at one point and a lizard as large as a fox at another, before coming across an astonishing ruin:

It is an enormous castle, fortress, palace—what you will—1555 metres x 170 metres, the immense outer walls set all along with round towers and about a third of the inside filled with court after court of beautiful rooms vaulted and domed, covered with exquisite plaster decoration, underground chambers, overhead chambers, some built with columns, some set round with niches, in short the most undreamt of example of the finest Sassanian art that ever was. It is not even in the map, it has never been published, I never heard its name before. . . . As soon as I saw it I decided that this was the opportunity of a lifetime.[61]

What Bell had discovered would become known as the palace of Ukhaidir. She spent several days taking photographs of the site, making notes, and drawing detailed plans of the castle. Then she headed on to the site of the ancient city of Babylon, where she observed the work of a group of German archeologists. From there, she traveled to Baghdad, spending a few days at the British consulate before once again going into the desert.

The German archeologists had helped her map out her route, and so, crossing the Tigris, she traveled north to the territory controlled by the Shammar tribe, to Mosul, and into the Kurdish mountains. It was here, in the small town of Khakh, that a crisis occurred.

Bell had made camp near the ruins of a fourth- or fifth-century church. In the middle of the night, she woke up to find a man in her tent. Ripping open the mosquito netting and jumping from bed, she chased after him, but he escaped. Only when she returned to her tent to put on some clothes did she realize that the stranger had taken her boots, some of her clothing, half of the contents of one of her trunks, some money, and, worst of all, her saddle bags. These had contained her two notebooks and the film of all the photographs she had taken. The work of four months had vanished with a thief in the night.

Bell sent frantic messages to the local authorities as well as to the Turkish administrator and the British consulate. Then she sat down and attempted to recreate from memory the contents of the two notebooks. After a week during which the authorities searched and Bell wrote, the thief was found and the stolen goods were returned to her.

As she prepared to return to England, one final disappointment awaited her. In Constantinople, while dining at the French embassy, she learned that she was not the first to discover and write about the palace of Ukhaidir. A French archeologist had reported his findings to a French journal, which had published them before she had arrived in Constantinople.

AMURATH TO AMURATH

Back in England, Bell spent the next year and a half writing about her travels, working on scholarly articles and on *Amurath to Amurath,* a book of her impressions of all that she had seen. Some time earlier, she had become involved in the Women's Anti-Suffrage League, a response to the movement to give women the right to vote that was sweeping across England, and she continued her activities in support of this cause.

Her involvement in the movement to deny women the right to vote seems to contradict sharply who she was— a strong, independent woman. Gertrude Bell was clearly a pioneer who demonstrated again and again that she was as capable as any man. Writer Janet Wallach suggested that Bell supported the antisuffrage movement because she earnestly believed that women were not equipped to run the country. While in the East, she enjoyed extraordinary freedoms; at home, she firmly adhered to tradition. Furthermore, she was horrified by the suffragettes' very public demonstrations: They chained themselves to public buildings and harassed the very public officials who were Bell's friends.[62] It was in part Bell's sense of herself as exceptional and extraordinary that led her to this conclusion; she clearly felt that although she might be equipped to comment on public policy and advise government officials, most women were not.

The reviews for *Amurath to Amurath* were not as glowing as those for *The Desert and the Sown*. Gertrude left England and spent some time studying antiquities in Rome before returning to the East in early 1911. She had decided to return to the palace of Ukhaidir, feeling that she might still obtain some research of archeological value there. Next, she decided to travel to Carchemish, in the hope of once more meeting with David Hogarth, but by the time she arrived, Hogarth had left the site. Bell decided to meet instead with his colleague, Campbell Thompson, who was overseeing work at the excavation site of the Hittite ruins.

She met Thompson and was introduced to his 23-year-old assistant, a short, quiet student named Thomas Edward Lawrence. In a letter home, Bell noted admiringly that Lawrence "is going to make a traveler," and indeed the young man who shared Bell's interest in the East would earn a reputation equal to her own. Eventually he would be known as "Lawrence of Arabia."

Bell returned to England in June and began work on her book on Ukhaidir. She hosted Major Doughty-Wylie in early 1913, when they were both in London, and she and the diplomat spent time together discussing the politics and events in the East. The Ottoman government was being challenged by a group of reformers known as the "Young Turks," and the British government was considering the opportunity this decline in Ottoman power presented in the Middle East.

DESERT PLANS

Bell spent a good deal of time with Doughty-Wylie. They had many shared interests, including a love of the East. She invited him to spend time with her family while his wife was traveling, and soon she realized that she was in love with him. He made it clear that he shared her feelings.

The two exchanged many passionate letters, but Bell felt a strong sense of what was proper and right, and although she might be in love with a married man, she could not act upon

THE YOUNG TURKS

The collapse of the Ottoman Empire happened over a period of years, sparked by the cumulative effect of many different events. The revolution led by the "Young Turks" proved that the empire could be challenged and that the climate was ripe for political change.

This revolution began in Salonica (now part of Greece), the headquarters of the Ottoman Third Army, when a secret society was formed. Known as the Committee of Union and Progress (C.U.P.), its members (many of them soldiers) swore loyalty only to the Koran and the gun (not to the Ottoman sultan). These soldiers were promoted and soon had weapons and soldiers under their command. Many of them had gone for months without pay, victimized by economic downturn in a collapsing empire whose ruler feared a military coup.

The C.U.P. did not want to create a new nation; its aim was to return the empire to the "good old days" when the military was powerful and the ruler was not corrupt. By 1908, its members had seized power and formed a new government. The Young Turks did not fully understand what they had put into motion. They used words like "Liberty, Equality, Fraternity, Justice"—revolutionary words they meant to apply to Turks. Bulgaria, Bosnia, Herzegovina, Crete, and other territories of the empire soon decided that the ideas behind these words applied to them as well, and they quickly moved to secure their own freedom from Ottoman rule.

The Ottoman elite soon found it impossible to maintain control. The C.U.P. would ultimately place its own military dictatorship in power in the capital—a government more corrupt than the one it had replaced. It was, in the end, a government that would witness the empire's final collapse.

her feelings. After several weeks, Doughty-Wylie wrote to Bell to tell her that he was being sent on a new assignment, this time to the Balkans.

Bell was now 45 years old. She had found a man she could love, a man who loved her in return but who could not offer her anything more. She decided to fight off her feelings of loneliness as she had before—by planning a trip to the desert. This time she was determined to travel to Arabia.

As Bell planned her journey, she received favorable reports of the situation in Arabia from Percy Cox and her other contacts in the region. They assured her that the time was finally right for her long-planned journey. The region was relatively quiet, they said, and the conflict between Ibn Rashid and Ibn Saud had abated. Thus, Bell departed for her first journey into the deserts of Arabia.

POLITICS AND INTRIGUE

As revealed in the first chapter of this book, the information Bell had been given proved false. Arabia, and indeed much of the Ottoman Empire, was not quiet. The Turkish rulers were being attacked on multiple fronts as various political groups formed to challenge authority or establish their own.

In 1908, the Young Turks had seized power in Constantinople, forcing the ruling sultan to resign and taking control of the government. The new government they formed was soon struggling financially. The cost of maintaining such a vast empire—and the military power necessary to police it—was enormous. As they searched for sources of money and aid to help prop up their government, they found several European powers eager to assist them in exchange for the opportunity to gain a foothold in the region.

One of these powers was Germany. Germany had long recognized the strategic importance of the region and was busily constructing a railroad line running from Baghdad to Berlin. German-Turkish ties were also strengthened by the fact that many of the Young Turks were graduates of Ottoman military academies run by German officers.

The British were concerned by the shifting alliances forming in the region. The Berlin-to-Baghdad railway was a particular concern, because it interrupted the trade route that led from India through the Middle East and on to England.

In addition, the British (like the Germans) were becoming increasingly aware of a new resource available in the Middle East: oil. By 1911, British naval forces had begun to switch their battleships from coal-burning to oil-burning engines. Great Britain was rich in coal but not in oil, and the vast supply of oil in the Middle East meant that the region was increasingly important to the British. Political unrest, a change in leadership, weakened states, and a growing German presence all represented a threat to the British government.

When Bell returned from Arabia, she spent time in Baghdad. She met the British consul there, a Colonel Ramsay, whom she found unimpressive. She considered him a poor choice at a time when politics in the region were so volatile. According to Bell, he knew nothing of the land where he was living. He spent the mornings sleeping and the afternoons playing cards, did not understand Turkey or Arabia, and did not speak a single foreign language. She was more impressed by Baghdad's Muslim leader, the Naqib, whom she had met once before. While she was in Baghdad, Naqib graciously met with her and shared the information he had on regional politics.

Bell then traveled to Damascus. In the desert, she came across the tents of Fahad Bey, the chief of the desert's noble Anazeh tribe. Fahad Bey treated her with kindness and hospitality. He offered her advice and the protection of one of his men as a guide in the now dangerous area. In turn, she shared with him the information she had gathered in Arabia and Baghdad.

In Damascus, she learned that Ibn Rashid's uncle, Ibrahim, whom she had met while being held in Hayil, had been murdered. She wrote to Sir Louis Mallet, the British ambassador in

Gertrude Bell in Her Own Words

A Letter by
Gertrude Bell

Gertrude Bell was a prolific letter writer and diarist during her life. Many of her letters and diaries remain today, offering primary accounts of a critical time in the course of history, particularly that of the Middle East. Although the letters she wrote home from the region were typically censored by the British government, Bell still managed to record many of the fascinating details of her day-to-day activities. In the following letter, written on April 27, 1916 from Basra, Bell writes to her stepmother about her work and provides us with a glimpse of her busy and remarkable life.

Dearest Mother. I missed the mail last week for I was out for a night at a little place on the edge of the desert called Zubair [Zubayr, Az] and when I came in I found that the confounded post had gone a day earlier than usual. So there it was. I've had no letters for nearly 3 weeks, except one from Lord Cromer last mail, forwarded by you. Your handwriting on the envelope was something but I shall be thankful if a rather more circumstantial communication turns up this week. It's possible that my post may have gone up the river since I see you addressed Lord C's letter c/o the A.C. and he is at the front. But I've registered my name at the post office to prevent any accidents of that kind. Nothing happens and nothing seems likely to happen at Kut [Kut, Al (Kut al Imara)]—it's a desperate business, Heaven knows how it will end. Meantime I have been having some very interesting work and as long as it goes on, I shall remain. One is up against the raw material here, which one is not in Egypt, and it is really worth while doing all these first hand things. I don't mind the heat—there has been nothing to speak of so far, the thermometre [sic] seldom about 90ø, and I rather like it. But I wish I had some clothes; my things are beginning to drop to pieces; I wonder if you are sending me out any, and if they will ever arrive! I think I shall write to Domnul in Bombay for some cotton skirts and some shirts. One wears almost nothing, fortunately; still it's all the more essential that that nothing should not be in holes. I have written to Mrs Shaw in Karachi and asked her to send me on anything that may come to me from home, Inshallah! I generally get up nowadays about 5.30 or 6 and when I haven't got to mend my clothes, bother them, I go out riding through the palm gardens and have half an hour's gallop in the desert which is very delicious. Then back to a bath and breakfast and across the road to G.H.Q. by 8.30, I work there till about 5.30 with half an hour off for lunch, after

B

which, if I haven't been out in the morning I go for a little walk, but it's getting rather too hot to walk comfortably much before sunset. Then I read a little or do some work which I have brought in with me, have another bath, dine at a quarter to 9 and go to bed. The days pass like lightning. Last week I went out for a night to Zubair. It's the funniest little desert place, something like Hail, 9 miles from Basra. The road was all under water and mud—Euphrates floods —till we reached the high edge of the real desert about a mile from the town. We have a political officer there, Captain Marrs, very nice and intelligent. I was put up at the post office in room with a mud floor furnished with my own camp bed and chair and bath and a table lent by Captain Marrs, but the shaikh of the town insisted on entertaining me and we went in to him for all our meals and unlimited gossip about the desert with which he is always in the closest touch since the caravans come in to Zubair. He lent us some horses in the afternoon and we rode out to Shaibah [Shu'aiba (Ash Shuaybah] where we have a small cavalry post. The officers took us round the battlefield, or part of it, and we galloped back to Zubair at sunset. After diner I paid a visit to the shaikh's harem. In the morning I photographed the town, lunched with the shaikh and drove back here. It was so nice to get above water level for a bit - in Basra we live in a swamp and the number of mosquitoes is really remarkable. Yesterday there came to see me a young man called Captain Young. He is doing political work here and is stationed a few miles up the river. He is a cousin of all those other Youngs and was with George Trevelyan in Serbia. He is doing very well here and is full of interest in his work. I am going to ride out to breakfast with him on Sunday to see some of his people—Arab people. Neither Aubrey nor the Admiral nor Mr Lawrence have come back—they go up river and disappear. I long for someone I know to come down so that I may hear what is happening for we get very little news. But I fear there is very little to tell. My friend Mr Dobbs, the Revenue Commissioner, has been away in India for 3 weeks' leave. He comes back tomorrow and I shall be very glad to see him. Sir Percy Cox is up river—I miss him too for I often did odds and ends of work for him. I'm very very glad I came here; it has been infinitely worth it.

I wonder how Maurice is. I'm much afraid he may be going back to France next month and the old anxiety will begin again. Oh I wonder how all my dear family is and wish for news. One falls into a kind of coma when one is so far away and wakes up with a jump at intervals. I shall leave this letter open till after the mail has come in.

C

During Gertrude Bell's first experiences with the Middle East, the Ottoman Empire still reigned in the region. This eighteenth-century map shows the region much as it appeared in the twentieth century under Ottoman Rule. However, the empire was growing weaker, and European leaders hoped to exert their influence on the Middle East to gain access to its valuable land, which was rich in oil and other natural resources.

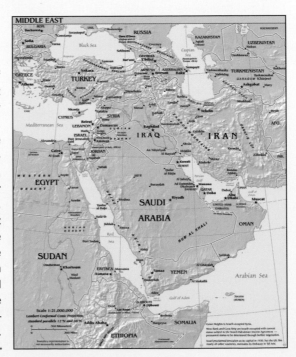

The identity of the Middle East changed drastically after World War I. New countries were formed, new leadership was assigned, and new power struggles emerged. Gertrude Bell spent much of her life working in the region to establish diplomacy and order during the tumultuous post–World War I era.

D

Bell reached Baghdad safely in 1914 after being held captive by the Rashid family. Although she did not consider her first journey to meet Ibn Rashid and Ibn Saud successful, she would eventually meet them both, and her ideas and negotiations would dramatically influence the development of the Middle East after World War I.

In 1913 and 1914, Bell began a journey to the Middle East hoping to meet with warring leaders Ibn Saud and Ibn Rashid. The journey was very dangerous, especially for a woman from Europe. Bell was held captive for several days in Hayil under orders from Ibn Rashid, before being escorted to Baghdad by the men in this photograph, preventing her from meeting with Ibn Saud.

During her time in the Middle East, Gertrude Bell formed a friendship with T. E. Lawrence, who shared her love of the region. Lawrence was a Welsh soldier and author who was a valuable resource for the British during World War I. He was dubbed "Lawrence of Arabia" after helping the Arabs revolt against the Ottoman forces and adopting the Middle East as his homeland.

With the end of World War I, leaders of all the European nations gathered at the Paris Peace Conference to decide, among other things, who would control the countries of the former Ottoman Empire. Here, King Faisal I of Iraq stands with T. E. Lawrence and other delegates.

F

Faisal I served as king of Iraq from 1921 until his death in 1933. Gertrude Bell was instrumental in Faisal's election, supporting him as a candidate at the Cairo Conference, and later educating him about Iraq and advising him during his rule.

In 1921, Britian's chief Middle Eastern representatives came together in Cairo to discuss the future of Mesopotamia. Winston Churchill led the conference, and in attendance were T. E. Lawrence and Gertrude Bell (the only woman). After several weeks of debate, borders were drawn and leadership was assigned for the region.

G

During his time as secretary of war and colonial secretary, Winston Churchill spent a significant amount of time analyzing the situation in the Middle East and facilitating the transition of the countries in the region from members of the Ottoman Empire to independent nations.

After growing up with his family in exile from Arabia, Ibn Saud vowed to reclaim his homeland. By 1932 he had done so, proclaiming himself king of the Arabian Peninsula and renaming his kingdom Saudi Arabia. Unfortunately, although Gertrude Bell argued that Ibn Saud would be an important ally for England, the British generally sided with his rivals and consequently suffered reduced access to oil and tense diplomatic relations with Saudi Arabia.

Constantinople, asking for a meeting and telling him that she had gathered information about Ibn Saud and Ibn Rashid in Arabia that he might find useful. He quickly responded that he would be happy to talk with her.

Bell arrived in Constantinople on May 13 and was soon writing from the British embassy there that Sir Louis had graciously received her and was grateful for the information she had. There were rumors of war, and British authorities were concerned that Turkey might ally itself with Germany in the event of a conflict.

Bell's travels had taught her that the Ottoman Turks were not firmly in control of much of their Arabian territory. Ibn Rashid and Ibn Saud were clearly attempting to gain their own control of the peninsula, and Bell had heard rumors that Ibn Saud might be interested in negotiating with the British in order to build an alliance that would help him in his attempt to rule Arabia. She had heard that the Arabs in Syria also might be interested in an alliance with Great Britain.

It was extremely valuable information, which Sir Louis dutifully conveyed back to his superiors in England. At his urging, Bell remained for a few days as his guest and then traveled back to England.

THE WORLD AT WAR

Bell was in England when she learned that Archduke Ferdinand, the heir to the Austro-Hungarian throne, had been assassinated in Sarajevo on June 28. A chain of events, sparked by simmering conflicts and alliances, quickly followed. Austria-Hungary declared war on Serbia; Russia responded by siding with Serbia and declaring war on Austria-Hungary. Germany sided with Austria-Hungary and was soon mobilizing troops, threatening France and England, which responded by mobilizing their troops and declaring war on Germany.

By August 1, 1914, the conflict that would later be known as World War I was underway. Battles were being fought across

Europe, and Turkey became even more strategically significant. British battleships needed to protect their oil supply as well as their trade route to India.

When Turkey sided with Germany, British officials did not forget the reports that Gertrude had passed on to them. She was asked to provide the director of British military intelligence in Cairo with a report of what she had seen and learned during her travels. In response, she sent him her ideas and recommendations, advising him that Syria, Iraq, Kuwait, and many in Arabia would willingly ally themselves with Great Britain.

The undertone of her report was clear: Parts of the Ottoman Empire were extremely weak and could be encouraged to revolt against the Turkish authorities. She asked for permission to travel to the region to assist in the war effort, an offer that was refused. She was, after all, a woman.

Eager to help, Bell began to give speeches throughout Yorkshire, encouraging people to support the war effort. She briefly volunteered as a nurse before being asked by Lord Robert Cecil, director of the Red Cross, to work with the organization in Boulogne, France. Her assignment was to help families that were trying to trace missing or wounded soldiers.

It was a new office, and when Bell arrived, she was disturbed by the chaos and confusion. She quickly organized her group, but it was difficult work. All too often, families had to be told that their loved ones were no longer alive or that no trace of them could be found at all. To her father, she wrote, "I sometimes wonder if we shall ever know again what it was like to be happy." [64]

She also wrote long letters to Charles Doughty-Wylie, who had been posted to Ethiopia. Bell had sent him her personal journals while she was traveling through the East, and he had praised her for her courage and spirit. Now, separated by war, the two exchanged letters full of longing. "Dearest dearest," she wrote in one, "I give this year of mine to you and all the years that come after it. Will you take it, this meagre gift—the year and me and all my thoughts and love." [65]

AN END AND A BEGINNING

In mid-February 1915, Doughty-Wylie wrote to Bell that he would be spending a brief period of time in England before taking on a new assignment. He stopped first in France, but they did not meet there. In a strange coincidence, Doughty-Wylie's wife Judith was also working in Boulogne—she had been sent there to serve as a nurse. Judith remained in Boulogne, nursing wounded soldiers; Doughty-Wylie traveled on to London.

Soon after, Bell met him in London, and they spent four days together. Her feelings for Doughty-Wylie were very strong, but she still held back. She struggled and suffered with the intensity of her feelings. Later, after he had left London, she wrote to him, trying to explain her unwillingness to betray the values that mattered to her, "Because I held up my head and wouldn't walk by diverse ways perhaps in the end we can marry. I don't count on it, but it would be better, far better for me." [66]

Bell returned to Boulogne and immersed herself in her work there. By mid-March, Doughty-Wylie had been sent to his next assignment, to serve in the British military forces that were preparing to attack Constantinople from Gallipoli. Bell, thanks to her efficiency in organizing the Red Cross's Boulogne office, had been assigned to the main office in London to bring the same efficiency to the operation there.

On May 1, while dining with friends, Bell learned that the British plans for a surprise attack at Gallipoli had been foiled. Turkish forces had spotted the landing party and had fired upon them as they attempted to reach the beach. Many British soldiers had been killed; Doughty-Wylie was among them. It was devastating news for Bell. She spent several days at Rounton, comforted by her father and stepmother and a few close friends. Once again, she had lost a man that she had loved. She sank into a depression, suffering from loneliness and a sense of isolation.

Eventually, she returned to work in London. Where once she had written long, detailed letters to friends and family, the few messages that she sent during this period were very brief. In one letter she poignantly noted, "I haven't anything to say that's worth, or at any rate worthy of saying, and therefore I don't write." [67]

In the fall, Bell received a summons from her old friend David Hogarth, who was working in the British intelligence service based in Cairo with T. E. Lawrence, the young archeologist Gertrude had met in 1911. Lawrence had been urging Hogarth and other British officials to work with Arabs, to encourage them to revolt against their Turkish rulers. This was the same suggestion that Bell had made earlier, and Hogarth quickly explained to his superiors that her knowledge of Arabia, Mesopotamia, and Syria would prove invaluable to their efforts.

On November 19, 1915, Bell set sail for Cairo. The journey was rough and stormy, but at its end she was met by Hogarth and Lawrence, who escorted her to her hotel and brought her up to speed on events in the region.

She was quickly put to work providing Hogarth with information on the Arab tribes and sheikhs. She loved the work and enjoyed working with Hogarth, who respected her intelligence and expertise. He was initially alone in this; the British Military Intelligence Office was staffed exclusively by an elite group of men who did not welcome the woman who confidently strode into their offices. Before Bell's arrival, Hogarth had written to his wife, "The military people here are much put about how she is to be treated and to how much she is to be admitted. I have told them but *she'll* settle that and they needn't worry!" [68]

Bell ignored the slights from her fellow staff officers. She had a right to be confident—she had valuable information, and her contributions would prove critical to British intelligence in the region. She was given a challenging project: categorizing the numbers and lineage of the various Arab tribes, data that would help determine who best could form an alliance with British forces and inspire other Arabs to revolt. The tone and tenor of Bell's letters home quickly changed; once again they were long, reflecting a woman who was in her element.

She reviewed the intelligence office's files, adding data from her travels. She made notes that reflected her firsthand observations, the connections and feuds between the various tribes, the strengths and weaknesses of the various sheikhs. When Arabs came into the office, she talked with them, and through these conversations gained additional information.

She formed a friendship with T. E. Lawrence, who shared her love of the East. She dined frequently with the chief British official in Cairo, Sir Henry McMahon, and his wife. Through their conversations, she learned that McMahon supported the idea of encouraging an Arab revolt.

Since mid-1915, McMahon had been in negotiations with Sharif Hussein of Mecca, who controlled the western region of Arabia and, in particular, the two holy cities of Islam—Mecca and Medina. He was one of the three most powerful men in Arabia (the other two were Ibn Saud and Ibn Rashid), and he was thought to be a descendant of Muhammad—a figure of tremendous religious importance not only in Arabia but in all places where the Muslim faith was practiced.

Bell understood the appeal of forming an alliance with Sharif Hussein, but she felt that he was not as strong militarily as his rival, Ibn Saud. She suggested that an alliance also be formed with Ibn Saud, and British officials agreed. Her advice proved valuable: Ibn Saud would one day conquer all of Arabia.

This, however, was in the distant future. Most British intelligence officers were gambling on Sharif Hussein to lead the Arab revolt. They encouraged him by implying that he would be rewarded for sparking a revolt: In return for his help, he would ultimately be given his own Arab kingdom. The question of where the borders of that Arab kingdom would be drawn posed some difficulties. Hussein wanted to rule over all

T. E. LAWRENCE

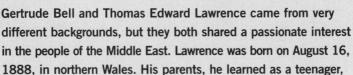

Gertrude Bell and Thomas Edward Lawrence came from very different backgrounds, but they both shared a passionate interest in the people of the Middle East. Lawrence was born on August 16, 1888, in northern Wales. His parents, he learned as a teenager, had never married. In fact, Lawrence's father was still married to another woman when he was born.

His family moved to England when Lawrence was eight. Bike trips to France and exploring Welsh castles sparked his interest in history and architecture.

Lawrence attended Oxford, and it was while he was a student there that he made his first trip to the Ottoman Empire—a walking tour of Syria, Palestine, and Turkey. For more than two months he explored the region, ultimately walking 1,100 miles. He returned to Oxford with treasures he had found or purchased and a reputation as an expert in the Middle East.

Lawrence later participated in archeological expeditions in the Middle East. He befriended Arabs and began to learn their language and customs. He became known for his ability to motivate Arab workers; when World War I broke out, his contacts made him a valuable resource for British authorities. He worked in the intelligence service, assigned to help with the planned Arab revolt against Ottoman forces.

Lawrence ultimately helped lead the revolt, wearing Arab clothing and earning a reputation for bravery. He later criticized Great Britain for what he believed were false promises to the Arabs and refused an honorary title from King George V.

His exploits in the Middle East made him a celebrity, and he was proud to be known as "Lawrence of Arabia," feeling more at home in his adopted homeland, the land he helped shape, than he ever did in Great Britain.

"Arabs" and requested a kingdom that would include not only the Arabian Peninsula but also Mesopotamia, Syria, and parts of Palestine.

This created a dual problem for the Cairo office. At the time, Syria was controlled by the French, and British forces in Mesopotamia (Iraq) were being directed by the British viceroy in India, who strongly opposed encouraging a revolt among the Arabs, particularly one directed by a Muslim leader. The largest Muslim empire in the world was the British Empire, but the millions of Muslims who lived in India were loyal to the Muslim holy leader based in Turkey: the caliph who served as the Ottoman sultan. Those Muslims would be loyal to Muslims in Turkey, not in Arabia. In addition, promising Mesopotamia to Sharif Hussein meant handing over control of its oil resources as well as a geographical point of strategic importance to India, Persia, and the Persian Gulf.

The differing positions soon sparked a clear conflict between the British offices in India and in Cairo. Each had its own ideas about how best to handle—and eventually administer—the Middle East. Their positions were dramatically different. The Cairo group believed that the simplest and most cost-effective solution was to create an Arab kingdom that contained Arabia and Mesopotamia. Officials in India felt that Mesopotamia should become part of the territory they administered and that there should be a strong, British-directed administration in Arabia.

The situation was even more complicated because the Cairo Bureau needed the support of the viceroy in India in order to proceed with the planned revolt. The viceroy had access to the funds—and the weapons—the Arabs would need for the revolt. There was, however, one person in the Cairo office that knew the viceroy and might be able to persuade him to change his mind: Gertrude Bell.

In January 1916, Bell wrote to her stepmother, noting carefully (to avoid the censors) that she might travel to India for a few days later that month. She said that she had received an invitation from the viceroy, "who wants to see me. It comes rather conveniently for there are certain matters on which we should like to have the V's sympathy and co-operation."

On January 28, she wrote another letter from Cairo, this time hastily noting that she was catching a troopship at Suez that same day. She had learned at 3:00 P.M. that space would be available for her if she could be ready by 6:00 P.M. In three hours, her things were packed, she had written to her father, and she was off, employed on a diplomatic mission that would dramatically affect the future of the Middle East.

6

Intelligence
Officer

In Delhi, Bell was quickly taken to meet with the viceroy, Lord Charles Hardinge. Lord Hardinge remembered Bell from Bucharest; he had also followed her career since then and knew that any information she could provide would be not only impartial but also valuable.

Bell's first meeting was with Hardinge; later, she met with intelligence officers and with officials in the Indian Foreign Affairs office. She explained her reasons for supporting the plan for an Arab revolt and found the viceroy receptive. Soon, plans were being put into place for greater cooperation between the Egypt and India offices to ensure that intelligence work was shared.

For three weeks Bell met with officials and discussed the events in the Middle East. One thing soon became clear: Mesopotamia would be an important strategic point for the war and what came after. Bell believed that Mesopotamia could be the launching point for an Arab revolt against Ottoman forces. The viceroy suggested that she travel to Basra to work with the British intelligence services based there.

Basra is located in the southeastern corner of the territory we now know as Iraq. It served as a critical port for Mesopotamia, linked by several waterways to the Persian Gulf. Its location also placed it close to the borders of Persia, Arabia, and Kuwait.

In sending Bell to Basra, Hardinge wanted her to do more than oversee the intelligence efforts there. He wanted her to meet with Arabs and gather as much information as she could about activities in the various parts of the Ottoman Empire. He wanted her to continue to link the efforts of intelligence teams in Egypt and India. He also wanted her to serve as a liaison with the Arabs to convince them to ally themselves with the British.

AT HOME IN MESOPOTAMIA

As Bell neared Basra, she was delighted to travel up the Euphrates and see the familiar landscape there—the palm groves, the Arab huts, the apricot trees. "I'm so glad to see it all again and I feel as if I were in my own country once more," she wrote to her father.[70] Whether or not there was a job for her to do was still uncertain.

Basra and the Mesopotamian territory around it had been seized from Turkish control in November 1914. It was now British Occupied Territory, with thousands of British soldiers visible in the streets, and the 33,000 Arabs who lived there were under British military rule, directed by Bell's friend Sir Percy Cox.[71]

Once more, Bell was treated coolly by the British intelligence staff. This time she had no specific job, or even a title, which did not improve her position. Staff members quickly made clear to her exactly what they thought of her. The woman who sauntered into general headquarters in her fancy dress and feathered hat would be put in her place: She would obey military rules, her mail would be censored, and she would be forbidden to enter any Arab homes without a chaperone.[72] She was not even given her own space to work; instead, she was provided with some files on Arab tribes and then given a small space in the bedroom of one of the officers.

Cox treated her kindly, although he was not particularly fond of the plans of the Cairo office to spark an Arab revolt. He particularly did not like the idea of offering Mesopotamia to Sharif Hussein in exchange for his cooperation. In spite of his feelings, Cox knew that good relations with the Arabs were critical, and he thought that Bell might be helpful in this regard. Bell soon proved useful to British military forces in the region, as well. They were planning to march to Baghdad, but they lacked local guides to help them avoid ambush and steer them swiftly north. They also needed maps of the region. As it became clear that Bell could provide them with both, the attitude toward her changed. She was moved to a new office space with a large, cool porch and plenty of room for her books and maps. There, she worked for several hours in the mornings and afternoons, taking a break for lunch. At sunset, she walked through palm gardens for nearly an hour before getting back to work for a few more hours. "We are now on the edge of important things and we hold our breath," she wrote to her father in March 1916. "If we don't succeed—it will be uncommonly awkward."[73]

British forces encountered resistance in Mesopotamia, and the Turks continued to battle fiercely to retain control of the territory. The war had seemed distant to Bell when she was based in Cairo and India, but in Basra, the impact of the fighting hit home. Rumors reached the intelligence service that the Arabs, discouraged by Great Britain's poor efforts in Mesopotamia, were beginning to waver in their support.

It was clear to Bell that she could make a valuable contribution. David Hogarth also wanted her for his team. He had been given the assignment of reorganizing the military intelligence office in Cairo and heading up the newly created Arab Bureau, and he wanted Bell's help. He sent T. E. Lawrence to Iraq, hoping that Lawrence could find a replacement for Bell there so that she could return to Egypt.

Bell spent a week with Lawrence before he traveled on to complete another mission, this one taking him to Kut, where he was to try to bribe Turkish officials to release the British soldiers they had captured. The mission would prove disastrous.

Bell wrestled with the idea of returning to Cairo. She preferred the work in Basra, where she believed she could be more useful. Her work in Basra was also more interesting and her contacts with Arabs more direct.

She asked her family to send additional dresses. As spring brought hot temperatures to Basra, she spent early all of her days indoors. Early in the mornings, around 5:30 A.M., she left her apartment to go horseback riding. The rest of day was spent inside. The doors and windows were kept shuttered to keep out the heat, but Bell found that the electric fans kept the rooms comfortably cool.

THE WINDS OF CHANGE

While the Arab Bureau searched for someone to replace Bell in Basra, its members reaching the conclusion that it might require two men rather than one, she continued serving as a liaison between activities in Basra and Cairo. The Arab Bureau had begun circulating a publication for high-level intelligence officers, providing them with an analysis of the personalities and politics of the region, and Bell's reports were frequently published in this *Arab Bulletin.*

Bell was also charged with making contact with Ibn Rashid to ensure his cooperation with British plans, and with continuing to provide analyses of local Arab sentiments and attitudes toward potential British plans. She traveled along the Euphrates River in the heat of the summer, gathering data and gossip that filled in many of the gaps in British intelligence.

Despite the value of the information she was gathering, Bell still lacked an official position and an official title, placing her in an awkward and uncertain position with the other members of the intelligence staff. Finally, Cox acknowledged Bell's hard work—and the value of the information she provided—by making her an official member of his staff. She was given the title Liaison Officer, Correspondent to Cairo, and a fixed salary, making her the only female political officer in Great Britain's forces.

In spite of this official recognition, frustration soon followed. Arab forces, led by Sharif Hussein, had begun an attack against Turkish forces in the Hijaz region of Arabia—an attack that was loudly criticized by the viceroy of India. At almost the same time, Bell learned that her efforts to build an alliance with Ibn Rashid had not proven successful.

She suffered occasional bouts of fever, but as summer drew to a close, it was an attack of jaundice that sent her to the officers' hospital. After several days during which she felt too weak to move, she slowly began to recuperate in the medical facility (a commandeered Arab home), resting on the porch and doing some work or reading and sleeping at night on the roof under the stars.

By the time she was well enough to return to full-time work, she learned that her reports on the Middle East situation had received high praise from officials in London. She took on

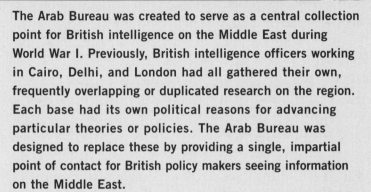

THE ARAB BUREAU

The Arab Bureau was created to serve as a central collection point for British intelligence on the Middle East during World War I. Previously, British intelligence officers working in Cairo, Delhi, and London had all gathered their own, frequently overlapping or duplicated research on the region. Each base had its own political reasons for advancing particular theories or policies. The Arab Bureau was designed to replace these by providing a single, impartial point of contact for British policy makers seeing information on the Middle East.

The Arab Bureau soon became involved in British efforts to gain control of the Middle East and protect British trade routes to India. The bureau's efforts to promote an Arab revolt with a leader handpicked by the British and to create British-friendly territories after the war ended sparked hostility. Arab Bureau staff efforts were directed at undertaking what they believed was their mandate—to support and protect British interests in the region. Many who were affiliated with the Arab Bureau—including Gertrude Bell and T. E. Lawrence—disagreed with this mandate and were strong advocates of Arab customs and culture.

At its formation in 1916, the Arab Bureau's goal was clear: to win the war and manage the peace.* Excessive expenses—in bribes and subsidies—and dissatisfaction with the outcome of bureau-sponsored policies in Syria, Palestine, and Arabia helped contribute to its closing in 1920.

* Bruce Westrate, *The Arab Bureau*, University Park, PA: The Pennsylvania State University Press, 1992, p. 7.

an even more important task: serving as an intermediary between Cox and the Arabs. The stress turned her hair gray, and soon it began to fall out in clumps. Still, she persevered.

Then came a meeting she had long anticipated. On November 26, 1916, Ibn Saud traveled to Basra, accompanied by Percy Cox. A difficult political juggling act was about to begin. Ibn Saud had become increasingly powerful in the Arabian Peninsula. The 40-year-old warrior was known for his courage and for his success in battle—even against incredible odds. He was also recognized for his skill at building alliances with the Arabian tribes and Bedouin warriors. He was not pleased at Sharif's statement that Great Britain had promised to make him the "King of the Arabs," and the British were concerned that Ibn Saud might attempt to prove his own power by attacking Hussein's stronghold at Mecca.

Percy Cox and British officials in India had long believed that if any one Arab should be chosen to lead the revolt against the Ottoman Empire, it should be Ibn Saud. Officials in London and Cairo had chosen to back Sharif Hussein instead, and now Cox hoped to keep Ibn Saud content by offering him money and weapons in exchange for a promise not to attack Sharif Hussein.

Cox wanted to impress Ibn Saud with British superiority. In Basra, Ibn Saud witnessed numerous examples of British power: a parade of armed forces, a display of antiaircraft fire, a demonstration of explosives, and a test flight of an airplane. He rode in a new motorcar and a new railway car. He was taken to a hospital and shown an X-ray of his hand.

There was something vaguely patronizing in all this, and the clever Ibn Saud felt it. Far more disturbing to him than the display of modern technology was the evidence of another dramatic difference between British and Arab forces: the presence of an unveiled woman who was not only allowed to approach him but was allowed to participate in the discussions and pepper him with questions.

Bell was constantly at Ibn Saud's side. Her Arabic was a classical version of the language, spoken in an accent that was quite foreign to him. Bell, perhaps unaware of how her presence in Cox's reception party unsettled Ibn Saud, described the Arab leader as "one of the most striking personalities . . . full of wonder but never agape."[74] In a later report for the Foreign Office, she continued her efforts to describe him adequately: "Politician, ruler and raider, Ibn Sa'ud illustrates a historic type. Such men as he are the exception in any community, but they are thrown up persistently by the Arab race in its own sphere, and in that sphere they meet its needs."[75]

Gertrude Bell's report was prepared and sent off, but she was frustrated by the limits placed on her because of her status as a woman. T. E. Lawrence had been allowed to travel with Sharif Hussein's army in Arabia. Accompanying Hussein's son, Faisal, Lawrence was witnessing first hand the earliest stages of the Arab revolt against Ottoman rule while Bell could only sit in her office and prepare reports. As she faced a cold, dark winter in Basra, depression began to sink in. She was battling a cold and feeling uncertain about what, if any, influence she could wield.

On December 9, 1916, she wrote to her stepmother:

I've been busy with a long memorandum about the whole of our central Arabian relations, which I've just finished. It will now go to all the High and Mighty in every part. One can't do much more than sit and record if one is of my sex, devil take it; one can get the things recorded in the right way and that means, I hope, that unconsciously people will judge events as you think they ought to be judged. But it's small change for doing things, very small change I feel at times.[76]

A NEW POST

Bell's reports sparked a new change in her status, and Percy Cox gave her a new place to live—a tiny suite of two rooms in the bureau's political office. She wrote to her family requesting a large quantity of clothes, both for winter and summer. She received one package, which arrived opened and missing the hoped-for clothing. She wrote again, this time expressing her concern that if she did not receive the needed clothes she would have to begin to wear Arab clothing instead.[77]

Bell found it difficult to work and felt frustrated with the little work she could manage. The seemingly endless war depressed her, yet she felt strongly that the British could not simply pull out of the region and abandon everyone and everything there. Her hair continued to fall out, and she noted that she might soon need a wig, because she did not even have enough hair to pin her hat to.[78]

Her spirits began to lift when her voluminous research on tribes and personalities of the region, gathered into a book titled *The Arab of Mesopotamia,* was published in early 1917. The book was published anonymously. Later, she would amusedly note that the reviews of her research on tribes frequently praised the scholarly man or men who had prepared it.

Bell went to work on another requested report, this one a contemporary history of Arabia for the intelligence service. She was approached about returning to work for the Arab Bureau in Cairo, but she did not want to leave Mesopotamia.

On March 10, 1917, British troops captured the city of Baghdad. Gertrude wrote to her family, noting that "We shall, I trust, make it a great centre of Arab civilisation, a prosperity; that will be my job partly, I hope, and I never lose sight of it."[79] Bell hoped to be called to a new post, this time in Baghdad, and her hope was soon answered. Percy Cox appointed her to the important intelligence post of Oriental Secretary, and she moved with him to Baghdad.

Bell's new position required her to serve as a kind of buffer between Percy Cox and the Arabs who came to his office. Her desk was literally just outside Cox's office. Here, she met with a wide range of people, all of them looking for answers from the new British administration in the city.

A HOME OF HER OWN

Cox had found a small home for Bell, but it was tiny and stifling, located in a dirty neighborhood, and lacking any furniture. She quickly decided that the hot little apartment would make her miserable and set out to find more suitable living quarters.

Not far from her rooms in the political office, she spotted a rose garden with three small summerhouses. It was owned by an acquaintance, and she quickly arranged to lease one of these. She added a kitchen, bathroom, and blinds to the house, and within five days, she was settled in her new home, surrounded by roses.

Bell visited all of her friends and contacts in Baghdad, making a special trip to meet with Abdul Rahman al Gailani, the city's elderly Naqib (the chief religious representative of Baghdad's Sunni Muslims). They had met before, and it was a sign of Bell's status in the city that she—an unveiled Englishwoman—was welcomed by the Naqib as an old friend.

Despite the intense heat, Bell was busy and happy. She woke early and went horseback riding. After bathing and breakfasting, she hurried to her office where she worked until 7:00 or 8:00 P.M. She met with tribal sheikhs and their representatives and summarized their concerns for Cox. She prepared tribal lists and maps and gathered all of the information she could, preparing detailed intelligence on Arab concerns and chief Arab personalities in Baghdad. In addition to her political duties, she was named Curator of Antiquities, responsible for overseeing and protecting the ancient mosques and sites in and around the city.

By mid-May, her letters were full of her love for Baghdad and her recognition of the importance of the work she was doing:

It's an immense opportunity, just at this time when the atmosphere is so emotional; one catches hold of people as one will never do again, and establishes relations which won't dissolve. . . . I want to watch it all very carefully almost from day to day, so as to be able to take what I hope may be something like a decisive hand in final disposition. I shall be able to do that, I shall indeed, with the knowledge I'm gaining.[80]

At the same time, Cox and Bell had learned of an agreement secretly signed by England and France in 1916. The Sykes-Picot Agreement specified the postwar carving up of the Ottoman Empire. Cox was furious at plans for Mesopotamia— he had wanted it to become part of India's territory, with Ibn Saud as its king. Instead, that title had been promised to Sharif Hussein, and Mesopotamia would be carved up into separate zones of influence.

Bell and Cox also learned that the Arab Bureau had settled on the man best suited to leading the Arab revolt. It was Faisal, the charming and courageous third son of Sharif Hussein.

By November 1917, Faisal's army was busy with a campaign of guerilla warfare against the Turks. His men sabotaged the Turkish railway that connected Medina, in Arabia, to Damascus, in Syria. They formed alliances with other tribes and captured city after city, providing a path for British forces into Syria where, Faisal had been promised, he would reign as king.

Bell's information—maps and tribal reports—was critical to the success of the Arab Revolt, and in 1917, she was honored for work. She was awarded the title Commander of the British Empire (C.B.E.), a titled bestowed only on those whose work for the empire was deemed significant.

MARK SYKES

Sir Mark Sykes played a critical role in forming British plans for the Middle East. Sykes was a wealthy baronet who was elected to the House of Commons in 1911. When he was seven, his father had taken him on a trip to the East, a trip that shaped a lifelong fascination with the region. He served for a time in the embassy at Constantinople and was the Conservative Party's Ottoman expert.

In 1915, he was assigned to the War Office, where he prepared information for troops serving in and around the Mediterranean. He became involved in a committee that was advising the cabinet on Middle East policy and was instrumental in outlining various options for the region: annexing the former Ottoman territories; dividing the territories into spheres of influence; leaving the empire in place but making the government ineffective; decentralizing the empire into small, semi-independent units.* The committee ultimately recommended the final choice, viewing it as the easiest. They created their own territories, outlining five provinces that would be autonomous but controlled by British influence.

Sykes was chosen to meet with the French representative, François Georges Picot, in November 1915, to negotiate the division of the Middle East. It was ultimately decided that France would control Lebanon and Syria. Control of Basra and Baghdad would go to Great Britain. Palestine was to be divided: the ports of Haifa and Acre, along with territory to construct a railroad to Mesopotamia, were given to Great Britain; an international tribunal was to govern the rest. The remainder of the Middle East was to be formed into Arab states, placed into either British or French zones of influence.

The Sykes-Picot Agreement was concluded on January 3, 1916. Sykes thought that he was following British policy; he would be surprised at the outrage the agreement sparked throughout the British Empire.

* David Fromkin, *A Peace to End All Peace*, New York: Avon Books, 1989, p. 148.

For a time, illness sapped her energy and prevented Bell from fully appreciating the honor, but by the spring of 1918, she had regained some of her energy and was focusing on a new task: drawing the boundaries between Mesopotamia and Persia. She felt a longing to visit Persia again, and in late June, she took a vacation. She spent a week in Tehran and a few more weeks camping in the mountains and countryside, gathering information for a new intelligence report on the country.

On her return to work, she was stunned to learn that Percy Cox was leaving. He had been reassigned to Persia and his replacement would be A. T. Wilson. Wilson was in his mid-30s, a brilliant politician whose relations with Bell were considerably cooler than those she had with Cox.

AN END TO WAR

On October 31, 1918, Bell received the welcome news that a peace agreement had been signed between the Allies and Turkey. Only a few weeks later, on November 11, she learned that the Allies had signed an armistice with Germany.

In the postwar excitement, British and French officials announced to the territories of the Ottoman Empire that they would be given the right to govern themselves. Rather than feeling reassured, the residents of these territories were alarmed. Who would rule them? How would these rulers be chosen? When? Gertrude Bell was besieged by anxious Baghdadis, all wanting answers.

She had been directed to assess local opinion—would Baghdadis prefer an Arab or British king? The response was not clear. Most, with the exception of the many Jewish residents of Baghdad, preferred an Arab king, but they could not agree on one candidate. At the beginning of 1919, Gertrude was still wrestling with this question and was busy gathering data for a book on prominent Iraqis.

7

A New
Nation

Gertrude Bell's next assignment from the Foreign Office was a significant one. Rough maps had been created in London, outlining the frontiers of the newly defined territories of Mesopotamia, Turkey, Persia, Syria, and Kuwait. Bell knew these territories intimately, so she added her own expertise to the mapmaking, correcting borders and boundaries and making sure that Mesopotamia contained the valuable territories of Baghdad, Basra, and Mosul. It was a heady responsibility. She was helping determine not only the shape of this new country—to be known as Iraq—but also making recommendations as to who would lead it, how it would be ruled, who its people would be, and what its laws would govern.[81]

Bell opposed the idea of an Arab king, believing that British rule would be best. Both Arab and British leaders, however, were demanding that the British prepare to phase out the military occupation of Mesopotamia, the Arabs out of a desire to see self-government delivered as promised and the British out of concern for the ongoing expense of maintaining a British presence in the region.

A. T. Wilson asked Bell to travel to London to offer her expertise to British policy makers, but her plans quickly changed. In Paris, representatives of the European nations were gathering to decide the fate of the Middle East and to carve up the Ottoman, Russian, and Austro-Hungary empires. Wilson wanted Bell in Paris to represent British interests in Mesopotamia.

PARIS PEACE CONFERENCE

Bell arrived in Paris on March 7, 1919. Leaders of all the European nations were there—each with an agenda. Great Britain wanted to maintain control of Mesopotamia, set up protectorates in Egypt and Persia, and take over German colonies in Africa and the South Pacific. Italy wanted parts of the Austro-Hungary Empire. France wanted Alsace and

Lorraine (then German territories), Syria, and other parts of the Ottoman Empire. Above all, everyone wanted access to oil.[82]

Faisal, accompanied by T. E. Lawrence, was also in Paris for these critical meetings. He was representing both his own interests and those of his father. He hoped to be named king of Syria; his father, Sharif Hussein, expected the British to honor their promise of giving him a kingdom stretching from Arabia to Iraq and north to Palestine, Syria, and Lebanon. Hussein planned to rule Arabia himself; he wanted Faisal to rule Syria and his oldest son, Abdullah, to rule in Baghdad.

Having promised Syria to Faisal (in their negotiations with Sharif Hussein) and to the French (in the Sykes-Picot Agreement), the British were now caught in an awkward position. Neither side wanted to give in.

Bell recommended to Faisal and his staff that he negotiate with the French. She knew that conditions in Syria were not good and that the British, caught in the middle, would not want to interfere. T. E. Lawrence had no intention of allowing Great Britain to renege on its earlier promises to Faisal. He had become one of Faisal's closest advisors and hoped to continue in that position when Faisal became king. When Lawrence learned of Bell's advice, he replied, "Miss Bell has a poor mind. You should not attach any importance to what she says."[83]

Lawrence soon decided to take a different approach and attempted to win Bell over to the group supporting Faisal. He spent hours walking, talking, and eating with her. Gradually, her opinion began to shift, and she moved toward supporting an Arabian head of state in Mesopotamia. A. T. Wilson arrived on March 20 and was horrified to learn that Bell no longer supported the idea of a British High Commissioner in Mesopotamia. She had earlier advised him that the differences between Arabia and Mesopotamia were too great for an Arabian to rule Mesopotamia: The regions shared little more than a religion. Now her opinion had changed.

Unable to reach a firm conclusion on Mesopotamia, the conference adjourned. Neither Mesopotamia nor Syria was given the right to self-rule; instead, the two territories were placed under British and French mandate.

AT HOME

Bell spent time with her father in France and Belgium, then traveled to London and on to Rounton. She had not been in England for four years, and she enjoyed the opportunity to rest and visit with family and friends. She was not in England long.

By September 1919, she was once more sailing for the East, traveling to Cairo, Jerusalem, and finally Damascus. Everywhere she went, she found hostility toward Great Britain for not honoring its promises—or what all believed had been promised. In Egypt, the anger was sparked by strong demands for self-government. In Palestine, Jews and Arabs were angered by Great Britain's wishy-washy policy on the creation of a Jewish homeland. She wrote presciently:

> There is practically no questions but Zionism is Jerusalem.
> All the Muslims are against it and furious with us for back-
> ing it and all the Jews are for it and equally furious with us
> for not backing it enough. Our attitude, meanwhile, is to
> halt between the two and wonder what to do for the best.[84]

Bell found Damascus dirtier and its people less friendly than on her last visit, but it was now operating under Arab control, under Faisal's rule, and she studied the evidence of Arab self-government with a careful eye. She then traveled on to Aleppo, where she met her old servant Fattuh. He had suffered under Turkish rule for his connection to a British political official; he had also lost his homes and most of his possessions. They reminisced about their desert journeys, and Bell sadly said, "Oh Fattuh before the war our hearts were so light when we travelled, now they are so heavy that a camel could not carry us."[85]

She returned to Baghdad to prepare her report on all that she had seen on her travels. The report, completed on November 15, 1919, revealed how dramatically her thinking had changed. Her conclusion that an Arab state in Mesopotamia might be desirable angered Wilson and most of the British working in the region. Wilson disagreed with Bell's proposal and made his disagreement clear. Bell was soon at odds with all of her colleagues and was given a chilly reception whenever she entered a room.

Despite the hostility, Bell continued to work to build a rapport with Shiite religious leaders, understanding that they held authority over many and that their anger toward the British could jeopardize any plan to build a new government in Mesopotamia. Her efforts were hindered by the refusal of these religious leaders to look upon an unveiled woman and by her refusal to bow to local practice by wearing a veil. "I think I'm right there, for it would be a tacit admission of inferiority which would put our intercourse from the first out of focus," she wrote.[86]

As the debate over the future of Mesopotamia continued, unrest in the region threatened the tenuous peace. Could a ruler from Arabia govern Mesopotamia, a region with very different customs and practices? Could anyone unify the educated urban residents of Baghdad (who were generally Sunni Muslims) with the nomadic tribes (who were generally Shiite Muslims)?

A NEW REGIME

In March 1920, Faisal was crowned king of Syria, and his older brother, Abdullah, was put forward as the leading candidate for king of Iraq. Bell sensed that the latter choice would prove disastrous. She knew that Abdullah lacked Faisal's diplomatic and military skills; she also knew he did not share Faisal's desire to rule. Abdullah's shortcomings did not concern British administrators, who were under intense pressure to bring an end to the large and expensive military presence in Iraq. The situation was further complicated by Great Britain's interests in the valuable Iraqi oil fields. Parliamentary debates centered on whether or not Great Britain needed to oversee the entire country or merely a few select parts of it.

Bell's father arrived in Iraq in late March. She was thrilled at the opportunity to show him the country she now considered her home, and his visit comforted her as she struggled with hostile colleagues. In spite of pressure, she remained firm in her support for determining a sensible outcome to the crisis, one based on Arab nationalist interests: ". . . if we leave this country to go to the dogs it will mean that we shall have to reconsider our whole position in Asia," she wrote to her stepmother. "If Mesopotamia goes Persia goes inevitably, and then India. And the place which we leave empty will be occupied by seven devils a good deal worse than any which existed before we came." [87]

On April 25, 1920, the San Remo Conference, between Great Britain's Lloyd George and France's Georges Clemenceau, marked a conclusion to the debate over Ottoman territories. France would govern Syria and Lebanon under mandate. Arabia would remain independent. Palestine and Mesopotamia would be governed under British mandate. Both France and Great Britain were to share Iraq's oil resources.

The news created chaos in the region. The people had been promised an opportunity to govern themselves, but it seemed that this promise was being honored only in Arabia. With the beginning of Ramadan, the Muslim holy month marked by fasting, religious leaders began calling for a *jihad* (holy war) against the British, ultimately hoping to set up an Islamic state. Riots and strikes soon followed.

The unrest deepened the chasm between Bell and her colleagues. She saw it as evidence that an Arab state should quickly be established; they viewed the violence as proof that an increased British presence was necessary to maintain peace.

Percy Cox returned briefly to the region, demonstrating his support for Bell and providing A. T. Wilson, her supervisor, with the authorization to call for a constitutional assembly as a first step toward building a new government in Iraq. Cox then left, promising to return to help set up the new government. The assembly was called, and various leaders arrived in Baghdad. Unrest continued outside the city.

Trouble was also threatening the peace in Syria. France refused to recognize Faisal's right to rule the region. In July 1920, he was forced to leave Damascus after less than two years of rule.

Bell's family was also facing a crisis. The Bell family fortune, built on iron and coal, had begun to slip away. Bell was forced to curtail her expenses and sign on to a bank loan to try and revive the family business.

In late September, A. T. Wilson left Baghdad. Bell felt a great relief at the departure of a man who had criticized her repeatedly and made her working life so miserable. In mid-October, Percy Cox returned, welcomed with great ceremony. It was a joyful reunion for Bell, particularly when Cox made it clear that he wished to proceed quickly with the plans for setting up a provisional government. He dismissed those officers who opposed his plans.

Cox's first step was to set up an Arab cabinet, with the Naqib serving as prime minister. It was a brilliant move, and soon other important figures joined the Naqib on the cabinet.

Bell met with Iraqis, preparing detailed reports and gathering intelligence from her many contacts. One of these noted that the British were going about things the wrong way by first setting up the foundations of a government and then working upward. "Begin with a roof," the man told her, "supported by a few pillars. The roof will encourage us to continue. Otherwise the slowness of building may discourage us. Give us a king. He will be our roof and we will work downwards." [88]

THE CAIRO CONFERENCE

There were many leaders who put themselves forward as the best candidates to lead the new nation. Bell believed that Faisal was the best choice. In her eyes, Faisal's military skills, his experience setting up a government in Syria, and his demonstrated political skills lifted him above all other candidates.

Rising unemployment in England made the issue of the expense of maintaining a military presence in Iraq more pressing. The crisis had become the responsibility of Secretary of State for War Winston Churchill.

In February 1921, Churchill called for Great Britain's chief representatives in the East to gather in Cairo to determine future policy in Palestine, Transjordan, and Mesopotamia. Bell was chosen to be part of the Mesopotamian delegation. She was the only woman among the 40 delegates.

The conference began on March 12, and Gertrude Bell found an ally for her beliefs in T. E. Lawrence. He and Bell pushed for an Arab government in Iraq led by Faisal. Churchill made it clear that he supported the move—a quick and relatively inexpensive solution—and the proposal was approved. The move also gave Great Britain greater leverage over both Faisal and his family—Sharif Hussein, who needed British subsidies and protection to fight Ibn Saud's forces in Arabia, and Abdullah, who was ruling in Transjordan.

The conference addressed the issue of how to emphasize Faisal's right to rule the Mesopotamian territory. Bell and Lawrence both noted that Faisal would need to emphasize his connection to the Prophet Muhammad. Faisal was a Sunni Muslim; a majority of Iraq's population was Shiite Muslim. Differences between Sunnis and Shiites (based, in part, on differing interpretations of who succeeded Muhammad after his death) might be bridged by the fact that Faisal was himself a descendant of Muhammad. Even though Faisal was currently in London, it was determined that he should travel first to the holy city of Mecca before being "summoned" by the Iraqi people to rule them.

At the end of the conference, on March 25, Bell deservedly felt triumphant. The borders she had drawn were becoming reality; now she could claim to have helped create a country's government and even pick its king. Iraq was taking shape exactly as she had imagined it.

THE ONCE AND FUTURE KING

Bell returned to Baghdad and quickly set to work paving the way for Faisal's acceptance without letting it be thought that Great Britain was backing one particular candidate. On June 12, 1921, Bell learned that Faisal had left Mecca and was on his way to Iraq. He arrived in Basra on June 23 and then traveled on to the Shiite holy cities of Karbala and Najaf before proceeding to Baghdad.

Faisal arrived in Baghdad on June 30. It was a grand occasion, with cheering crowds waving Arab flags. He was formally welcomed to the city by Cox and other British officials, including Bell. To her dismay, Bell soon learned that his hearty welcome in Baghdad had not been mirrored at earlier stops. His election was far from certain. Crowds in Basra, in Karbala, and in Najaf had been indifferent or, in some cases, hostile. Worse still, Faisal was receiving mixed signals from British officials about whether or not they would support him.

Bell met with Faisal and assured him that he had Cox's support as well as her own. She knew that he could win Baghdad and Mosul. The rest was less certain.

This trip was Faisal's first time ever in Iraq. He did not know the land or its history. He even spoke a different version of Arabic—a mixture of Hijaz, Egyptian, Syrian, and Turkish.[89]

On this issue, Bell could help. She met with Faisal frequently, explaining the geography and history of the land he was to rule. She introduced him to sheikhs, religious leaders, and all the important people she knew. Bell worked diligently, understanding that she was making history. She was frequently exhausted by the endless conferences and formal receptions and dinners, all held in scorching temperatures. ". . .You may rely upon one thing—I'll never engage in creating kings again; its too great a strain," she wrote to her family.[90]

Bell was able to persuade the Naqib to meet with Faisal and accept him as king of Iraq. She even persuaded the leaders of Baghdad's large Jewish population to welcome Faisal. They gave a grand reception, and, at Bell's prompting, Faisal rose and said, "There is no meaning in the words Jews, Muslims and Christians in the terminology of patriotism. There is simply a country called Iraq and all are Iraqis."[91]

Faisal even won the support of the desert tribes. Accompanied by Bell, he met with tribal horsemen on the bank of the Euphrates River and announced that he was their brother and friend. He vowed to guard their honor as they swore allegiance to him.

Within five weeks, the cabinet had approved Faisal as their choice for king. By August 14, the people followed their lead. The question of whether or not they wanted Faisal to be their ruler was answered "yes" by approximately 96 percent of those voting.[92]

It was a happy time for Bell. She met constantly with Faisal, advising him and accompanying him on visits to various parts of the kingdom. He promised her that she would have her own regiment in his army—the "Khatun's Own" (Bell had become known throughout Baghdad as "El Khatun," or "The Lady").

She wrote to her family of a significant conversation with Faisal. She had joined him at his rented home, where he was enjoying the sunset on the roof. *"Enti Iraqiyah, enti badawiyah,"* he said to her. "You are an Iraqi, you are a Bedouin."[93]

The acknowledgment of her status and the recognition of her place in her adopted home mattered tremendously to Bell, but she worried constantly. The colonial office had notified Cox that Faisal, in his coronation speech, must announce that the British High Commissioner was the ultimate authority in Iraq. "It is I suppose difficult for them to realise that we are not building here with lifeless stones," Bell wrote in frustration. "We're encouraging the living thing to grow and we feel it pulsing in our hands. We can direct it, to a great extent, but we can't prevent it growing upwards. That is, indeed, what we have invited it to do." [94]

Early on the morning of August 23, 1921, the 36-year-old Faisal was crowned king of Iraq before a crowd of 1,500, including representatives from all of the different groups living within the borders of the newly defined country. A 21-gun salute marked the ceremony, and a band played "God Save the King." Iraq did not yet have its own national anthem.

Bell wasted no time in setting to work on the next important matter—designing Iraq's flag. Her choice was the flag of Hijaz (Faisal's family crest) with a gold crown on a red triangle. She sent her father a sketch of the design, asking for his comments. She had helped choose Iraq's king. Now she looked forward to helping him rule.

8

Stateswoman
and Advisor

Gertrude Bell played a critical role in the early days of Faisal's reign. He consulted her constantly, asking her advice on how to deal with threats from Ibn Saud in Arabia, who best should serve on his council, and how to settle tribal feuds.

She relished her position as advisor to the king. One of Faisal's advisors told her, "One of the reasons you stand out so is because you're a woman. There's only one Khatun. . . . So for a hundred years they'll talk of the Khatun riding by."[95] Bell was certain he was right.

They made a striking contrast—the handsome young king, garbed in flowing robes, and the middle-aged Englishwoman in frilly dresses and hats, armed with a parasol to guard her skin from the sun. Faisal asked Bell to arrange dinner parties for him, hoping that she would invite important leaders to cement his position as ruler. Concerns about the loyalty of the Kurds in northern Iraq sent Bell on a trip into Kurdish territory. She was then drafted by Percy Cox to define the borders between Iraq and Arabia. It was hoped that this step would eliminate the simmering discord between Ibn Saud and the various members of Faisal's family.

It was exhausting work, and Bell occasionally fell ill, but she was aware of all that she had accomplished and rejoiced in it. "It's shocking how the East has wound itself around my heart till I don't know which is me and which is it," she wrote to her father.[96]

Hugh Bell traveled east to meet with his daughter in April 1922. Gertrude climbed aboard one of the British air force mail planes and flew to Amman, in Transjordan, where she joined her father. They were invited to dine with the king, Faisal's brother Abdullah, and then they traveled through Transjordan, Palestine, and Lebanon.

Bell returned to meet with Faisal and report on her travels. She told him that she was convinced that Iraq was the only Arab country on the right path and that failure would mean "the end of Arab aspirations."[97]

THE QUESTION OF MANDATE

A conflict was soon simmering between Faisal and the British government. In order for Great Britain to sign a treaty of independence with Iraq, Faisal was expected to sign a document agreeing to British authority in the form of a mandate. Winston Churchill, serving as colonial secretary, felt that the mandate was critical to help Great Britain maintain control of Iraq's finances and foreign policy. Faisal felt that the treaty must give Iraq full independence.

Soon extremists were demonstrating against the mandate—and the British. Bell was disappointed that Faisal did not denounce them. In fact, Faisal soon announced that he could not support the mandate. He made it clear to Bell that he knew Great Britain had abandoned him in Syria, refusing to honor promises made. He had no confidence that the same would not happen in Iraq and was determined to build an independent Arab government.

Bell grew frustrated. She watched Faisal wavering between pro-British and extremist advisors and listened to him make promises that she knew he would not honor. By August 1922, she was complaining to her father of exhaustion—both physical and political. The air was humid and heavy, with temperatures well above 100° Farenheit. Bell wrote, "Every two or three days I get up in the morning wondering why, instead of getting up, I don't lie down and die." [98]

She and Faisal discussed plans to collaborate on a history of the Arab revival, and this pleased Bell, but she sometimes felt like a "prisoner." [99] She was 54 years old. She had helped shape Iraq and had played a critical role in the country it had become. Now, however, she could sense that Great Britain's role in Iraq was quickly coming to an end.

A NEW ERA

A compromise between Faisal and the British government was reached at last. Churchill made it clear that he would do his best to get Iraq admitted to the League of Nations. Once Iraq became a member, the mandate would no longer be in effect and Iraq would be an independent state. Faisal accepted the compromise. On October 8, 1922, he signed the treaty and forwarded it to the national assembly for approval.

Bell was now working closely with a new British intelligence officer, Ken Cornwallis. Cornwallis had served in the Arab Bureau and headed the Cairo intelligence office. He had also served as Faisal's advisor in Damascus. He had earned Faisal's trust, and Faisal had insisted that Cornwallis be posted to Iraq to assist him.

Cornwallis was intelligent. As he and Bell spent more and more time together, serving as Faisal's official advisors, she grew to respect and admire him.

In addition to her other duties, Bell was appointed as the honorary Director of Antiquities. She became involved in regulating excavations, in working with archeologists, and in overseeing the cataloguing of ancient treasures.

In spite of her achievements and honors, Bell's political influence was beginning to wane. Faisal no longer relied heavily on her counsel, eager to distance himself from the British officials in his country. Cox was planning to leave Iraq, and Bell debated whether or not she would remain after his departure. "Seven years I've been at this job of setting up an Arab state," she wrote in January 1923. "If we fail it's little consolation to me personally that other generations may succeed, as I believe they must." [100]

In May 1923, Percy Cox left Iraq. Shortly after his departure, Bell decided to go to England for a vacation. When she returned to Routon, however, she found that the home she had known no longer existed. The Bell family fortune had been greatly diminished. Portions of the estate were closed off and the size of the staff had been reduced to save money.

Bell decided to return to Iraq but was uncertain about what she would find there. She knew Cox's successor, Henry Dobbs, but he did not have Cox's stature or the shared history Bell had enjoyed with Cox. She was also aware of her growing attraction to Ken Cornwallis (the British intelligence officer she had worked with when she was last in Iraq), despite the fact that he was 17 years younger than she was. He was also married.[101]

Bell returned to Baghdad in September. She found Dobbs easy to work for, but there was no longer much for her to do. She helped Faisal furnish his palace, asking her family to help her obtain some stamped leather for his throne.

In November, she oversaw the inauguration of the American School of Archeology and met with archeologists and anthropologists who arrived in Baghdad to help get the school launched. She was there when Faisal celebrated the opening of a new railway to Kerbala. She inspected the work being done at important archeological digs, marching through rain and mud when her car broke down and happily sleeping in a tent on the desert sites. The dig at Ur, the 6,000-year-old Sumerian city, would yield detailed treasures giving a complete picture of Sumerian life—golden headdresses, daggers and statues, towers with staircases still intact, curved canoes, and tablets marked with cuneiform.

TRACES OF HISTORY

As her political role diminished, Bell focused more and more on the idea of building a museum to house the great artifacts being uncovered in Iraq. Any treasures uncovered must, by law, first be offered to Iraq—a law that Bell had drawn up to protect the country's rich heritage. Thanks to this law of excavation, many important pieces were collected for Iraq's museum. Bell worked in the museum's temporary quarters, overseeing workers, cataloguing objects, and supervising the painstaking handling of antique fragments. She also was appointed to serve as head of the Salam Library—the only European ever elected to the position—and helped establish an Iraqi branch of the Red Cross.

The treaty with Great Britain was ratified by the Iraqi National Assembly in June 1924. Then, as summer heat descended on the city, many of Bell's colleagues—including Cornwallis—left. Cornwallis had gone to England to settle his wife's request for a divorce. Dobbs went to Egypt. Bell spent a difficult birthday, suffering through 121° Farenheit heat and blasting winds.

Her workload was now so light that she often spent only a few hours in the morning at the office before returning to her home to lie under a fan and read. She was lonely, had lost her appetite, and soon became sick. By late August, she couldn't leave her bed, battling illness and depression.

Gradually, she recovered, and by fall she felt well enough to meet the king's son, 12-year-old Ghazi. Faisal had hesitated to bring his family to Baghdad, but now their home in Mecca was facing the threat of attack from Ibn Saud and his forces. Bell presented Ghazi with a toy train and was delighted by his joy as he watched it move along the rails.

Bell also met Faisal's wife and daughters when they arrived in December. She busied herself with helping the queen settle into her new role and met with the League of Nations' commission to verify the borders between Turkey and Iraq. She assisted with negotiations over oil between the Iraqi government and a consortium of British, French, and American interests known as the Turkish Petroleum Concession.

Nevertheless, her importance was diminishing. She did not always agree with Dobbs, complaining that his poor Arabic made him incapable of quickly grasping political nuances. She frequently upstaged Faisal at official events, angering him when she turned up uninvited.

In July, Bell left for England, hoping to rest. She was thin and weak and knew that there was little left for her to do in Iraq but still less for her in England. Her parents were moving from Rounton—the estate had become too expensive to maintain. A friend suggested that she run for Parliament, but she dismissed the idea.

Bell returned to Iraq in October. It was a sad homecoming. She had asked Cornwallis to marry her before her trip to England, but he had refused. Now, back in Baghdad, she pleaded with him to change his mind. She wrote to her stepsister, "After I came back we had some terribly bitter talks. . . . So now I'm bent on showing him what he really knows, that he can't do without me."[102] She threatened to leave Iraq if he wouldn't marry her, knowing that a life in England without him would only be a kind of "half life."[103]

SAD FAREWELLS

Bell spent Christmas battling a bad cold. Summoned by Faisal to join him at his country estate, she put on several layers of clothes and traveled with the king and Cornwallis by trolley, riding with a hot water bottle on her knees. She was so ill that Cornwallis sent back to Baghdad for a doctor who diagnosed pleurisy (an inflammation of the membrane that covers the lungs and lines the chest). Slowly, she recovered.

Within a month, Bell received the sad news that her brother Hugo had died. He had contracted typhoid while traveling from South Africa to England with his wife and children and lost his battle with the illness on February 2, 1926.

Bell tried to busy herself with work. Her relationship with Cornwallis had deteriorated into a "comforting" friendship; she had no connections to the newer and younger British staff members in Iraq. She still had lunch with Dobbs every day, but it was clear that she was no longer at the center of action.[104] Her work with the High Commissioner was coming to an end. She hoped to be selected for a temporary position as the director of the Iraqi museum, perhaps for six months. She considered another trip home, to spend the summer in England, but decided against it, worried about the expense.

The Baghdad Museum officially opened to the public on June 16, 1926. King Faisal attended the opening ceremony, and Bell was pleased to see groups of Iraqis touring the collection.

She had collected more than 3,000 artifacts and was still cataloging them after the museum opened.

Although pleased that the museum was a success, she was still battling depression. She wrote to her stepmother:

> It is being a very grim world, isn't it. I feel often that I don't know how I should face it but for the work I'm doing and I know you must feel the same. I think of you month after month as the time passes since that awful sorrow [her brother's death], and realize all the time that the passage of months can make little difference. . . . But it is too lonely, my existence here; one can't go on for ever being alone. At least, I don't feel I can. . .[105]

Her father urged her to come back to England, but she refused, saying that she was too busy with the museum. "Give me a little time to get things into some kind of order," she pleaded, noting that, "Except for the Museum work, life is very dull."[106]

The July heat further sapped her energy, making it difficult for her to write long letters home. She took photographs of the museum and sent these to her family instead of words.

On July 11, 1926, Bell ate lunch with Henry Dobbs and another colleague. She tried to go swimming later, but the heat and strong undertow in the river tired her. She left a note for her maid, asking to be awakened at 6:00 A.M. the next morning. Then she took an extra dose of sleeping pills and went to sleep.[107] She never awoke.

FINAL WORDS

Whether or not Bell intended to commit suicide was debated throughout Baghdad. The official report stated that she had died of natural causes, and her stepmother, in the collected *Letters of Gertrude Bell* that she edited, explained that the heat and workload were too much for Gertrude: "She died quite peacefully in her sleep."[108] Friends and colleagues knew that she had frequently battled depression, and her servant admitted to a British official that she had taken an extra dose of her sleeping pills.[109]

Bell had served her native country and her adopted homeland well, and on July 12, 1926—two days before her fifty-eighth birthday—she was given a full military funeral. She was buried in the city she had loved, honored by the many Iraqis whose lives she had touched, the entire staff of the British High Commissioner, the Iraqi Army, the Iraqi prime minister, and his Arab cabinet.

The King of England sent a message to her parents, providing a fitting epitaph for Gertrude Bell's rich life:

> The nation will with us mourn the loss of one who by her intellectual powers, force of character and personal courage rendered important and what I trust will prove lasting benefit to the country and to those regions where she worked with such devotion and self-sacrifice.[110]

In the museum she helped found, a plaque honoring her memory was installed:

GERTRUDE BELL
Whose memory the Arabs will ever hold in reverence and affection
Created this Museum in 1923
Being then Honorary Director of Antiquities for Iraq
With wonderful knowledge and devotion
She assembled the most precious objects in it
And through the heat of the Summer
Worked on them until the day of her death
On 12th July, 1926
King Faisal and the Government of Iraq
In gratitude for her great deeds in this country
Have ordered that the Principal Wing shall bear her name
And with their permission
Her friends have erected this Tablet.

Chronology

1868 Gertrude Bell is born on July 14.

1871 Bell's mother dies.

1876 Bell's father marries playwright Florence Olliffe.

1886 Bell begins classes at Oxford.

1888 Bell graduates from Oxford, becoming first
woman ever to earn a First in Modern History;
travels to Romania.

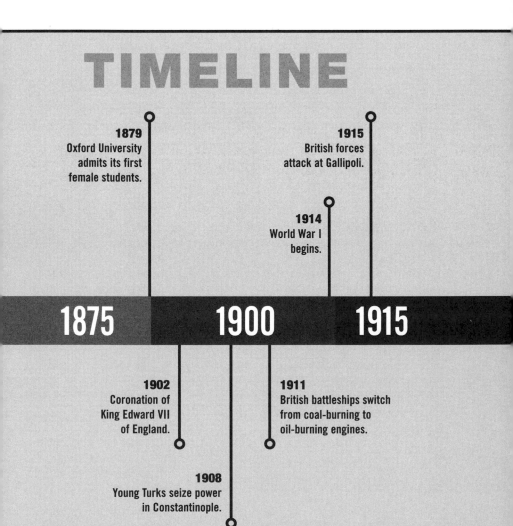

TIMELINE

1879
Oxford University
admits its first
female students.

1915
British forces
attack at Gallipoli.

1914
World War I
begins.

1875 **1900** **1915**

1902
Coronation of
King Edward VII
of England.

1911
British battleships switch
from coal-burning to
oil-burning engines.

1908
Young Turks seize power
in Constantinople.

1889 Bell travels to Constantinople.

1892 Bell travels to Persia.

1894 *Persian Pictures* is published.

1897 *Poems from the Divan of Hafiz* is published.

1899 Bell meets archeologist David Hogarth;
climbs 13,081-foot-high Grand Pic de la Meije;
travels to Palestine.

1916
Sykes-Picot Agreement
is signed.

1920
San Remo Conference
is held; Iraq is
mandated to British.

1918
Armistice signed;
World War I ends.

1924
Treaty of Independence
between Great Britain
and Iraq is ratified.

1916   1920   1932

1919
Paris Peace
Conference
is held.

1921
Cairo Conference
is held; Faisal is
crowned King of Iraq.

1917
British troops capture Baghdad.
Arab Revolt marked by guerilla
warfare against Turks.

1932
New kingdom of Saudi Arabia
(ruled by Ibn Saud) is created,
uniting the Arabian Peninsula
into a single monarchy. Iraq is
admitted to the League of Nations.

Chronology

1900 Bell journeys into Druze territory.

1901 Bell climbs Mount Engelhorn.

1902 Bell travels to Malta and Haifa; climbs Mount Wellhorn and Finsteraahorn in Switzerland.

1905 Bell travels to Syria.

1907 *The Desert and the Sown* is published; Bell travels to Asia Minor to collaborate with William Ramsay on archeological digs; meets Charles Doughty-Wylie.

1909 *The Thousand and One Churches* is published; Bell travels to Mesopotamia.

1911 *Amurath to Amurath* is published; Bell meets T. E. Lawrence.

1913 Bell begins travels in Arabia.

1914 Bell completes Arabian travels; World War I begins; Bell works in Red Cross office in Boulogne, France.

1915 Doughty-Wylie is killed in British attack at Gallipoli. Bell leaves for Cairo to join British intelligence service.

1916 Bell joins intelligence staff in Basra, Mesopotamia; meets Ibn Saud.

1917 *The Arab of Mesopotamia* is published; Bell is named Oriental Secretary and transferred to British political office in Baghdad; Bell named Commander of the British Empire (C.B.E.).

1919 Bell attends Paris Peace Conference.

1921 Bell attends Cairo Conference; Faisal becomes king of Iraq.

1923 Bell begins plans for museum to house Iraqi artifacts and antiquities.

1926 Baghdad Museum opens to the public. Bell dies on July 12.

Notes

Chapter 1

1. Janet Wallach, *Desert Queen*, New York: Anchor Books, 1996, p. 99.

2. Quoted in Gertrude Bell, *The Letters of Gertrude Bell*, vol. 1, ed. Florence Bell, New York: Boni and Liveright, 1927, p. 314.

3. Quoted in Gertrude Bell, *Diaries*, February 2, 1914, archived at University of Newcastle, downloaded from The Gertrude Bell Project, *http://www.gerty.ncl.ac.uk*.

4. Ibid., February 4, 1914.

5. Ibid., February 16, 1914.

6. Ibid., March 8, 1914.

7. Ibid., March 26, 1914.

Chapter 2

8. Gertrude Bell, *The Desert and the Sown*, New York: Cooper Square Press, 2001, p. 1.

9. Wallach, *Desert Queen*, 7.

10. Gertrude Bell, letter dated 12 July 1874, The Gertrude Bell Archive: The Letters, *http://www.gerty.ncl.ac.uk/letters/l1.htm*.

11. Ibid., 9 August 1876.

12. Ibid., 15 August 1876.

13. Quoted in Bell, *Letters*, vol. 1, p. 9.

14. Wallach, *Desert Queen*, p. 20

15. Quoted in Bell, *Letters*, vol. 1, p. 11.

16. Wallach, *Desert Queen*, p. 24.

17. Quoted in Bell, *Letters*, vol. 1, p. 12.

18. Ibid.

19. Quoted in Wallach, *Desert Queen*, p. 25.

20. Quoted in Ronald Bodley and Lorna Hearst, *Gertrude Bell*, New York: The Macmillan Company, 1940, p. 23.

21. Ibid., pp. 28–29.

22. Wallach, *Desert Queen*, p. 30.

23. Quoted in Bell, *Letters*, vol. 1, pp. 25–26.

Chapter 3

24. Ibid., p. 26.

25. Ibid.

26. Quoted in Bodley and Hearst, *Gertrude Bell*, p. 39.

27. Ibid., p. 42.

28. Quoted in Wallach, *Desert Queen*, p. 35.

29. Quoted in Bodley and Hearst, *Gertrude Bell*, p. 50.

30. Wallach, *Desert Queen*, p. 37.

31. Ibid., p. 39.

32. Quoted in Bell, *Letters*, vol. 1, p. 30.

33. Ibid., p. 49.

34. Ibid., p. 51.

35. Ibid., p. 58.

36. Ibid., p. 67

37. Ibid., p. 71.

38. Ibid., p. 81.

39. Ibid., p. 84.

40. Ibid.

41. Ibid., p. 87.

42. Ibid., p. 91.

43. Ibid., p. 108.

44. Ibid., p. 120.

Notes

Chapter 4

45. Ibid., p. 125.

46. Ibid., p. 133.

47. Ibid., p. 144.

48. Ibid., p. 148.

49. Quoted in Wallach, *Desert Queen,* pp. 67–68.

50. Quoted in Bell, *Desert,* pp. 1–2.

51. Quoted in Bell, *Letters,* vol. 1, p. 174.

52. Quoted in Bell, *Desert,* p. 11.

53. Ibid., p. 13.

54. Ibid., p. 23.

55. Ibid., p. 60

56. Ibid., p. 92.

57. Ibid., p. 139.

58. Ibid., p. 340.

59. Quoted in Bell, *Letters,* vol. 1, pp. 249–250.

60. Wallach, *Desert Queen,* p. 85.

Chapter 5

61. Quoted in Gertrude Bell, letter dated 26 March 1909, The Gertrude Bell Archive: The Letters, *http://www.gerty.ncl.ac.uk/letters/l862.html.*

62. Wallach, *Desert Queen,* p. 82.

63. Ibid., p. 126.

64. Quoted in Bell, *Letters,* vol. 1, p. 357.

65. Quoted in Wallach, *Desert Queen,* p. 137.

66. Ibid., p. 140.

67. Quoted in Gertrude Bell, letter dated 11 June 1915, The Gertrude Bell Archive: The Letters, *http://www.gerty.ncl.ac.uk/letters/l1099.htm*

68. Quoted in Wallach, *Desert Queen,* p. 147.

69. Quoted in Bell, *Letters,* vol. 1, p. 362.

Chapter 6

70. Ibid., p. 369

71. Wallach, *Desert Queen,* p. 158.

72. Ibid., p. 159.

73. Quoted in Bell, *Letters,* vol. 1, p. 372.

74. Quoted in Wallach, *Desert Queen,* p. 187.

75. Ibid.

76. Quoted in Bell, *Letters,* vol. 1, p. 390.

77. Ibid., p. 395.

78. Ibid., p. 398.

79. Ibid., p. 400.

80. Quoted in Bell, *Letters,* vol. 2, pp. 410–411.

Chapter 7

81. Wallach, *Desert Queen,* p. 215.

82. Ibid., p. 223.

83. Ibid., p. 227.

84. Ibid., p. 237.

85. Quoted in Bell, *Letters,* vol. 2, p. 470.

86. Ibid., p. 484.

87. Ibid., p. 486.

88. Quoted in Wallach, *Desert Queen,* p. 287.

89. Ibid, p. 312.

90. Quoted in Bell, *Letters,* vol. 2, p. 610.

91. Quoted in Wallach, *Desert Queen*, p. 314.

92. Bodley and Hearst, *Gertrude Bell*, p. 217

93. Quoted in Bell, *Letters*, vol. 2, p. 619.

94. Ibid.

Chapter 8

95. Ibid., p. 622.

96. Ibid., p. 632.

97. Ibid., p. 639.

98. Ibid., p. 646.

99. Ibid.

100. Ibid., p. 664.

101. Wallach, *Desert Queen*, p. 352.

102. Ibid., p. 367.

103. Ibid.

104. Ibid., p. 369.

105. Quoted in Bell, *Letters*, vol. 2, p. 770

106. Ibid., p. 773.

107. Wallach, *Desert Queen*, p. 372.

108. Quoted in Bell, *Letters*, vol. 2, p. 775.

109. Wallach, *Desert Queen*, p. 373.

110. Quoted in Bell, *Letters*, vol. 2, p. 777.

Bibliography

Books:

Bell, Gertrude. *The Desert and the Sown.* New York: Cooper Square Press, 2001.

————. *The Letters of Gertrude Bell.* Edited by Lady Florence Bell. 2 vols. New York: Boni and Liveright, 1927.

Bodley, Ronald and Lorna Hearst. *Gertrude Bell.* New York: Macmillan, 1940.

Fromkin, David. *A Peace to End all Peace: The Fall of the Ottoman Empire and the Creation of the Modern Middle East.* New York: Avon Books, 1989.

Kedourie, Elie. *England and the Middle East: The Destruction of the Ottoman Empire, 1914–1921.* Boulder, CO: Westview Press, 1987.

Klieman, Aaron S. *Foundations of British Policy in the Arab World: The Cairo Conference of 1921.* Baltimore, Md.: Johns Hopkins Press, 1970.

Mackey, Sandra. *The Saudis.* Boston: Houghton Mifflin, 1987.

Read, Donald. *England 1868–1914.* New York: Longman, Inc., 1979.

Wallach, Janet. *Desert Queen.* New York: Anchor Books, 1996.

Westrate, Bruce. *The Arab Bureau: British Policy in the Middle East, 1916–1920.* University Park, Penn.: The Pennsylvania State University Press, 1992.

Wilson, Jeremy. *Lawrence of Arabia.* New York: Atheneum, 1990.

Websites:

Archives Hub
http://www.archiveshub.ac.uk

English Heritage
http://www.english-heritage.org.uk

Royal Geographical Society
http://www.rgs.org

University of Newcastle Robinson Library: Gertrude Bell Project
http://www.gerty.ncl.ac.uk

Further Reading

Books:

Bell, Gertrude. *The Desert and the Sown*. New York: Cooper Square Press, 2001.

————. *Gertrude Bell: The Arabian Diaries: 1913–1914*. Syracuse, N.Y.: Syracuse University Press, 2000.

Lacey, Robert. *The Kingdom*. New York: Harcourt Brace Jovanovich, 1981.

Polk, Milbry and Mary Tiegreen. *Women of Discovery*. New York: Clarkson Potter, 2001.

Stewart, Desmond. *T. E. Lawrence*. New York: Harper & Row, 1977.

Websites:

Distinguished Women of the Past and Present:
Gertrude Margaret Lowthian Bell
http:// www.distinguishedwomen.com/biographies/bell.html

Newcastle University Library Special Collections Exhibitions.
Gertrude Bell Exhibition
http: //www.ncl.ac.uk/library/speccoll/exhibbell1.html

Smithsonian Magazine: Daughter of the Desert
http://www.smithsonianmag.com/smithsonian/issues98/apr98/bell.html

University of Newcastle Robinson Library: Gertrude Bell Project
http://www.gerty.ncl.ac.uk

Index

Index

Index

Index

Index

Picture Credits

Contributors

Heather Lehr Wagner is a writer and editor. She earned a B.A. in political science from Duke University and an M.A. in government from the College of William and Mary. She has written several books on the creation of the modern Middle East and is also the author of *Mary Kingsley* in the WOMEN EXPLORERS series.

Series consulting editor **Milbry Polk** graduated from Harvard in 1976. An explorer all her life, she has ridden horseback through Pakistan's Northwest Territories, traveled with Bedouin tribesmen in Jordan and Egypt, surveyed Arthurian sites in Wales, and trained for the first Chinese-American canoe expedition. In 1979, supported by the National Geographic Society, Polk led a camel expedition retracing the route of Alexander the Great across Egypt.

Her work as a photojournalist has appeared in numerous magazines, including Time, Fortune, Cosmopolitan and Quest. Currently she is a contributing editor to the *Explorers Journal*. Polk is a Fellow of the Royal Geographic Society and a Fellow of the Explorers Club. She is the also the author of two award-winning books, *Egyptian Mummies* (Dutton Penguin, 1997) and *Women of Discovery* (Clarkson Potter, 2001).

Milbry Polk serves as an advisor to the George Polk Awards for Journalistic Excellence, is on the Council of the New York Hall of Science, serves on the Board of Governors of the National Arts Club, the Children's Shakespeare Theater Board and is the director of Wings World Quest. She lives in Palisades, New York, with her husband and her three daughters. She and her daughters row on the Hudson River.